COMMERCIALIZING WOMEN

Images of Asian Women in the Media

THE HAMPTON PRESS COMMUNICATION SERIES
Women, Culture and Mass Communication
Karen Ross & Marjan de Bruin, *Series Editors*

COMMERCIALIZING WOMEN

Images of Asian Women in the Media

edited by

Katherine T. Frith
Southern Illinois University

Kavita Karan
Nanyang Technological University, Singapore

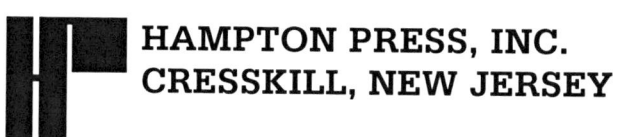

HAMPTON PRESS, INC.
CRESSKILL, NEW JERSEY

Printed in the United States of America
Library of Congress Cataloging-in-Publication Data

Commercializing women : images of Asian women in the media / edited by Katherine T. Frith, Kavita Karan.
    p. cm. -- (The Hampton Press communication series. Women, culture and mass communication)
    Includes bibliographical references and index.
    ISBN 978-1-57273-852-2 (hardbound) -- ISBN 978-1-7273-853-9 (paperbound)
1. Women in mass media. 2. Mass media-Asia. I. Frith, Katherine Toland. II. Karan, Kavita.
    P94.5W652A783 2008
    302.2.23082--dc22

                      2008017234

Hampton Press, Inc.
23 Broadway
Cresskill, NJ 07626

For Giles and Sebastian
(K.T.F.)

For Dr. Shiv Raj Mathur & Maya Devi
(K.K.)

CONTENTS

ACKNOWLEDGMENTS

This book would not have been possible without the assistance of many individuals and institutions. This project was launched in the School of Communication and Information at Nanyang Technological University, whose financial support in the form of a generous research grant underscores their commitment to issues of scholarship and diversity. In addition, as scholars we have also been fortunate to have an excellent network of colleagues who contributed their wealth of knowledge to the chapters in this book.

We also must thank our families for their contributions. We thank our parents who always encouraged us to strive to achieve the highest possible goals, and we thank our husbands, Ravi and Michael, who have cheered us up when the task seemed daunting and cheered us on with their good humor and editorial expertise.

And finally, we thank our series editors, Karen Ross and Marjan de Bruin. Their insightful comments have helped us shape and form this work. We would like to convey our gratitude and thanks to all of the people who have helped us create this book.

ABOUT THE CONTRIBUTORS

Katyayani Balasubramanian is the market research manager of a leading Indian telecommunications service provider. She currently handles all the consumer research carried out by the company. Katyayani has an MA in Journalism from The Ohio State University. Prior to this assignment, she has worked with The Gallup Organization in Mumbai, India and for a the public opinion research firm of Belden Russonello & Stewart in Washington, DC.

Hong Cheng, PhD, is an Associate Professor of Advertising at the E. W. Scripps School of Journalism at Ohio University, USA. His teaching and research interests center on international and cross-cultural advertising. He has published in *Gazette, International Journal of Advertising, Journal of Advertising Research, Journal of Communication, Journalism and Mass Communication Quarterly,* and *Sex Roles,* among others. He formerly taught at Bradley University, Illinois, and was a senior fellow (2002-2003) at Nanyang Technological University, Singapore. He is a former head of the International Communication Division of the Association for Education in Journalism and Mass Communication. He is also an Associate Editor of the *Asian Journal of Communication.*

Katherine T. Frith, EdD, is an Associate Professor, School of Journalism, Southern Illinois University. She has also taught at Nanyang Technological University in Singapore and previously was Chair of the Advertising and Public Relations program in the College of Communications at Pennsylvania State University and was a Fulbright Scholar in Malaysia and Indonesia. Before becoming an academic Dr. Frith was an advertising copywriter in New York for J. Walter Thompson, N.W. Ayer, DDB and Grey Advertising. Her books include: *Advertising in Asia: Communication, Culture and Consumption* (1996), *Undressing the Ad: Reading Culture in Advertising* (1998), and *Advertising and Societies: Global Issues* (2004).

Kavita Karan, PhD, teaches at the School of Communication and Information, Nanyang Technological University, Singapore. Dr. Karan received her PhD form the London School of Economics and a M.Phil and Master's in Communication and Journalism from Osmania University, India. She was the former Head, Department of Communication and Journalism, Osmania University, Hyderabad. She has investigated various issues in advertising, particularly those of gender, culture, new technologies, health, and children. She has presented papers at various international conferences and contributed chapters in books and journals. Her current research focuses on issues in advertising, health communication, internet and women, and culture in advertising.

Kwangmi Ko Kim, PhD, is an assistant professor of mass communication and communication studies at Towson University, where she teaches advertising-related courses. She received her PhD from Pennsylvania State University. She is also advisor to the Towson chapter of the American Advertising Federation, a student-oriented advertising club. Her research has been focused on the globalization of the advertising industry, particularly on the Asia-Pacific region. Her articles and book chapters have been published in *International Journal of Advertising, Asian Journal of Communication, Mass Communication and Society, Advertising in Asia: Communication, Culture, and Consumption, Terrorism, Globalization and Mass Communication.* She is currently, working on a comparative study to analyze U.S. and Korean newspaper coverage of cigarette trade talks. Her recent chapter, "Global Advertising in Asia," will be published in a book, *Communications Media, Globalization and Empire.*

Siddiqua Ovais is currently working as a Manager, Marketing Communications, at the German Institute of Science and Technology, Singapore, overseeing the planning and implementation of public communication strategies for the organization. She has two masters' degrees in mass communication, from Nanyang Technological University Singapore (2004), and from the University of Karachi, Pakistan (1992). Earlier she worked as a copywriter with affiliates of McCann Erickson in Pakistan, and Ogilvy & Mather and Leo Burnet.

Ping Shaw, PhD, is a professor and a director in the Institute of Communications Management at National Sun Yat-sen University, Taiwan. She received her PhD in mass communication from the Pennsylvania State University, USA. Her research interests include gender representation in media and transnational advertising. She has published articles in *Journal of Communication, Sex Roles, Media History, Asian Journal of Communication,* and other communication publications.

K. Viswanath, PhD, is currently a member of the faculty at the Harvard School of Public Health and the Dana Farber Cancer Institute, and a co-leader of the Health Communication Core of the Dana Farber/Harvard Cancer Center. Prior to his arrival at Harvard, Dr. Viswanath was the associate director for behavioral research and a senior health communication scientist at the National Cancer Institute, National Institutes of Health, Washington, DC. Dr. Viswanath received his PhD and MA from the University of Minnesota, Minneapolis, after completing graduate and undergraduate studies at Osmania University, Hyderabad, India. He has published extensively in the areas of health communication, communication campaigns and international communication.

Guofang Wan, PhD, is an associate professor at Ohio University, USA. She taught at Bradley University in Illinois and Shanghai International Studies University in China. She holds a PhD degree in curriculum and instruction from Pennsylvania State University, an MA in International Studies from the University of Warwick, United Kingdom, and an MA in English from Shanghai International Studies University. Her research interests include media literacy studies, cultural sensitivity, and the use of technology in education. She also has a longtime interest in how children and women are portrayed in media. She has published a number of journal articles and a book and presented at national and international conferences in all these areas.

1

COMMERCIALIZING IMAGES
OF ASIAN WOMEN

An Overview

Katherine T. Frith

Kavita Karan

Over the past thirty years, the bulk of research on gender has been conducted in the United States and Europe, and thus the literature reflects some assumptions about women that may be culture- or region-specific. In Asia, unlike in Western countries, systematic analysis of the images of women in the media has been limited. Fung (2000) contends that feminist liberal philosophy has not yet been internalized by women in Asia. Thus, this collection of essays greatly adds to our understanding of how women are being depicted in the commercial media across Asia.

In this collection, the authors examine the part that culture, religion, and philosophy play in media representations of women in Asia. Asia is especially interesting to study because Asian cultures are derived primarily from Hindu, Buddhist, Confucian, Moslem, and Taoist influences; thus the roles of women in these societies are distinctly different from those of women in the West, where Judeo-Christianity forms the basis of the dominant cultures.

In addition to the traditional forces that shape representation of women in the media, globalization has had a profound effect on media representation in Asia. Since the 1980s, an explosive growth in the number and influence of global media vehicles has occurred in the region, accompanied by a huge increase in the volume of persuasive messages in print, broadcast, and the new media. These messages often involve women. In fact, women are increasingly making their presence felt by becoming more involved in the media and as a growing target market by virtue of their earnings in the Asian workplace.

Thus, this book is intended to stimulate discussion about the depictions of women in Asian media by drawing attention to how women's images are being used and abused in media portrayals in advertising, as well as showing how these representations relate to the cultures and diverse historical legacies of these nations. In this collection, the authors focus on several influential and representative Asian countries: China, Korea, Taiwan, Singapore, India, and Pakistan. By sampling these countries, our contributors explore and compare among the underlying issues that affect the commercial representation of women in the region.

This book consists of a collection of original essays that draw meaning from the authors' closeness to the media cultures in their respective Asian countries. A range of methodologies are used to broaden our understanding of the representation of women in advertising from the point of view of message producers who see Asian women as a growing market for clothing and beauty products as well as from the point of view of many Asian women who see these commercial messages as tools for either subjugation or empowerment.

In this overview chapter we shall examine some of the underlying philosophical and cultural contexts that shape the life experiences of women in Asia: the influence of Confucianism in China, Korea, Taiwan, and Singapore; the traditional Hindu beliefs that have shaped life for women in India; and finally the role of Islam in constructing social norms for women in Islamic countries such as Pakistan. Together these traditional influences, along with the new and emerging global cultural values inherent in the media, weave a set of conditions that create the context for images of women in Asian media.

COMMERCIALIZING WOMEN— THE ASIAN LANDSCAPE

The way the media portray women has been an issue of much debate and contention for decades. Commercial images of women have generally reflected their secondary status, and women's roles depicted in these images are often defined by patriarchal attitudes. Though globally women's overall social and economic status has improved significantly over the past half a century, age-old gender biases against women still remain strong in many Asian countries. This constitutes a major barrier to women's advancement in social status towards the full equality with men that is a hallmark of democracy. This enduring bias is often reflected (and, to some extent, affected) by the portrayal and representation of women in the media—most particularly in advertising.

However, a general shift is evident in the way women's images are being projected in Asian commercial communication. Following leads from the West, Asian women are gradually emerging from their secondary status, factored largely by evolving social policies, increased levels of education, and a widening access to the media. These advances are beginning to be reflected in the media. Another significant factor has been the proliferation of global beauty products and the accompanying images of women using these products in advertising. One potent outcome is that women are increasingly being depicted not merely for sheer exploitation and commercialization, but as tools of independence and emancipation. Across Asia women are shaking off their stereotypical portrayals as submissive, traditionally attired, shy, neglected introverts or hard-working housewives. Today, as they model products in advertising—portrayed as trendy, carefree, and even in some countries in sexual roles wearing Western clothes—for better or worse, they are invading what was once the reserved territory of Western and Caucasian women models.

Each chapter in the book reflects a country's historical and social practices and delves into the traditional attitudes derived from religions and philosophies that frequently relegated women to a secondary status. Some of these traditions compared women and men to heaven and earth, considering men gods and women their slaves. Of course, modern attitudes have evolved and today, to a greater or lesser degree, each of these countries has given women active roles in their drive for development. This gradual process has induced a measure of emancipation and political participation. Yet, as some authors show, oppressive ideas still linger on in certain sectors of some countries.

The chapters on China, Korea, Singapore, and Taiwan highlight the similarities in their cultural norms. The chapter on Pakistan reflects interesting details of the norms and practices shared by many Islamic countries while pointing out the diverse cultural and political issues that differ in the roles women are allowed to play in these countries. The chapters on India reflect the strengthening trends in women's commercial portrayals under the influence of accelerating social, economic, and political changes. Together, this collection draws on a multiplicity of research techniques to study the commercial images of women across Asia.

CONFUCIAN TRADITIONS

In "Holding up Half of the 'Ground'? Women Portrayed in Subway Advertisements in China," Hong Cheng and Guofang Wan examine one of the newer advertising media being used in China. The tagline "Women hold up half of the sky" has been used for promoting and celebrating women's liberation in the country; and the authors use an ironic inversion of this to head their examination of the portrayal of women and men in subway advertising. The public spaces in China's subway systems are the latest of the new milieux for advertising, and ads in these spaces have the potential of attracting the millions of commuters in China's major metropolises who use subways as the primary means of daily transportation to and from work. For this study, the authors personally collected and analyzed hundreds of subway ads in subway stations in Beijing, Shanghai, and Guangzhou—currently the three main advertising markets in mainland China.

Cheng and Wan found that Chinese subway advertisements closely follow the current international trends in gender portrayal, and the ads were mainly targeted to young, predominantly female, consumers. They found this substantiated by the fact that women were portrayed more often than men in that many ads promote cosmetics and other personal care products for women. In an apparent attempt to ensure the attention of young women, Chinese subway advertising frequently used female models. However they were often used in stereotypical ways, portraying the women either as fulfilling family duties or dressed seductively in nonoccupational roles.

They observed that Chinese women models were used to advertise home appliances, cosmetics, and personal products, whereas male were most often used in ads for clothes, information, and entertainment. Thus, subway advertising resorts to some of the same stereotypes commonly seen worldwide in advertising.

The irony of portraying women in subway advertising either in family roles or dressed seductively in nonoccupational roles did not escape the authors' notice. They suggest that the advertising planners must have somehow overlooked the fact that females exposed to advertising on the subway are working women—precisely because it is while commuting to work that women see these ads. Cheng and Wan find that rather than adequately engaging young working women, these ads reinforce traditional and sometimes dysfunctional stereotypes.

In "Being a 'Good' Woman in Korea: The Construction of Female Beauty and Success," Kwangmi Kim reflects on the roles of South Korean women in a country in transformation from its traditional Confucian origins into a more modern, "open", Westernized society. She argues that despite Korea enjoying the status of a newly industrialized country, the overall status of women there continues to be low. This is in spite of women's enormous economic contribution. In fact, she argues, that by providing cheap and prolonged labor from the 1970s through the 1990s, women have helped push the country to its current economic heights.

Kim shows that women's roles in Korean society remain rooted in the rigid gender roles of Confucian philosophy. Traditionally, the husband was metaphorically referred to as "heaven," to signify his superiority, and his wife (as "earth") was supposed to serve him with reverence. However, despite the continuing rigid social structures and norms, she finds that Korean society is undergoing gradual changes in values. Some of these changes are manifested in shifting consumption habits and a gradual change in the physical appearance of the younger generations (mostly in the twenties and thirties).

Western influences on the portrayal of beauty and the appearance of new beauty and personal products seem to have brought about these changes in the consumption habits and personal presentation of Korean women. The author traces these influences to increased overseas travel as well as through the forces of globalization on the society as a whole and on the media in particular.

Despite these liberalizing influences, Korean women's magazine ads still use Caucasian models more frequently than local models when portraying sensuality in ads for women's intimate wear and personal care products. Thus, foreign models are used to express more liberal attitudes to young Korean women. She questions whether the tendency of Korean advertising to project Western beauty as superior to traditional Korean beauty might be responsible for insecurity in Korean women.

The imported beauty ideal has become so crucial among young Korean women that they are willing to spend fortunes having plastic surgery on their noses, eyes, and jaws. Growing numbers of young women are having their noses lifted, their jaws shaved, and their eyes widened in a drive to attain the Western image of beauty. Most recently, the author reports, young Korean women are using plastic surgery on their calves in the hope of obtaining the "Barbie" legs sported by the world's supermodels.

To augment her historical analysis of Korea's transformation, Kim uses content analysis to show that these changes are reflected in women's images depicted in leading Korean magazine advertisements.

Ping Shaw's "Women as Targets: Internationalization of the Women's Magazine Industry in Taiwan" first explores the growing concentration of ownership and control of the women's magazine industry in Taiwan. Then the author focuses on the increasing internationalization of Taiwan's women's magazines. These two trends, she argues, have resulted in the commodification of the audience, the magazine content, and of the industry as a whole.

Despite being somewhat politically isolated, Taiwan is rapidly developing into an international capitalist state whose strong economic growth has created a swelling, affluent middle class that attracts the attention of multinational consumer product giants.

As an advertising medium, transnational periodicals have become more powerful than domestic women's magazines in Taiwan through the extensive use of high-quality printing techniques, high-quality paper, glossy covers, and sophisticated advertising techniques.

Through their dominance, transnational magazines in Taiwan have established the model for all other women's publications in the country by establishing imported stereotypes of women in aesthetic roles that follow the Western beauty ideal of fashion conscious individualists, using luxury brands, and consuming beauty products. Portrayals of women as aesthetic objects, Shaw points out, have become one of the most profitable stereotypes used in Taiwan's magazine ads, and transnational advertisers have repeatedly found that this stereotypical portrayal successfully sells their products through local as well as transnational magazine advertising.

Ping Shaw employs a systematic content analysis of advertisements in two domestic women's magazines and two Chinese-language editions of international titles published in 2003. Her study shows that over three-quarters of all advertisements in the four titles were for products of transnational corporations. These products typically find their greatest appeal among the magazines' target audience: urban middle- and upper-class women who have the greatest purchasing power. In terms of Taiwan's social psychological development, the reader is drawn to speculate on the long-term impact of systematically portraying the "ideal" woman as individual-centered and materialistic, and as an adherent to a consumption-based Western lifestyle.

A more disturbing trend pointed out by Shaw is the blurring of the line between the advertising and editorial content of Taiwan women's magazines. The larger advertisers are wielding so much influence over editorial content that there is a danger of women's magazines losing their readers' trust as a result of their diminishing objectivity.

Ping Shaw's study is of particular interest to the developing international magazine industry in Asian countries. As women's magazines continue to attract the interest of transnational media conglomerates looking to profit from the huge Chinese-language market in Taiwan, China, Hong Kong, and Singapore, this study presents a further opportunity for research into the impact of the internationalization of the magazine industry on local women's culture.

Katherine Frith's study, "Commercializing Beauty: A Comparison of Global and Local Magazine Advertising in Singapore," builds on Shaw's work and examines how the beauty ideal is constructed in advertising in local and global editions of women's magazines published in Singapore. Historically, Singapore has traditionally been a predominately Chinese society with the same Confucian principles that structure other countries in Greater China. These are the Five Cardinal Relations (*wu lun*), "those between ruler and subject, father and son, elder brother and younger brother, husband and wife, and friend and friend" (Bond, 1986, p. 215). In each case, the senior member is accorded a wide range of prerogatives and authority with respect to the junior. Thus, although the rights of women in Singapore society are enviable to many women in developing countries across Asia, there are still strong patriarchal influences on roles women can play in society.

As one of the most globalized countries in Asia, Singapore is an interesting country to study. The population of Singapore is approximately 70% Chinese, and Mandarin is widely spoken here; it is also one of the most Westernized countries in Asia. English is Singapore's official language and this country is now host to a wide variety of international media. Special country editions of women's magazines such as *Elle, Cosmopolitan,* and *Harper's Bazaar,* are now published each month in special Singapore editions. In her chapter, Frith compares the portrayals of beauty in local and global women's fashion and beauty magazines sold in Singapore to help identify and understand the differences in the ways advertising in global media and local media construct concepts of feminine beauty. In particular, she finds that given the liberal media environment in Singapore, advertisers tend to use Caucasian models far more than local Asian models in both local and global women's magazines. She suggests that the overuse of Caucasian models in advertising in Singapore could be related to the high degree of globalization in this nation, or that it may be a trend that will emerge throughout Asia as the global women's magazine industry enters more developing markets. She also notes that local magazines feature more beauty products, whereas global women's magazines have a higher proportion of clothing ads. She suggests that beauty in countries such as Singapore may be related to face. Historically, when women are displayed in Chinese art it is the face and the hair that are the focus for beauty. Thus, the high proportion of ads for beauty products in local magazines may be indicative of the Singaporean woman's interest in skin and facial beauty.

HINDU TRADITIONS AND
THE MODERN INDIAN WOMAN

Kavita Karan, in "Visual Portrayal of Women in Media: Modern Indian 'Stereotypes,'" focuses on the gradual change in the portrayal of women in India. Historically, in Indian society women have been subservient to men. Although Hinduism *per se* does not relegate women to second-class status, the interpretation of some Hindu beliefs has historically shaped the roles and opportunities for women in Indian society. However, Karan notes that in advertising there has been a shift from the traditional portrayals of Indian women as submissive, shy, and introverted to more modern roles and representations. The author adopts various existing theoretical assumptions about the issues of concern to construct common traits in the visual portrayal of women and their representation in advertisements. Literature on the representation of women in India has been interesting and extensive, yet conflicting. In this chapter, therefore, she considers the many arguments that have emerged from the literature review without passing on their merits or demerits.

By means of an analysis of the content of advertisements in leading Indian women's magazines, the author analyzes the portrayal of women in various beauty types, roles, and poses, and correlates these with the products being advertised to explain the gradual modernization of the image of Indian women. Today, in Indian magazine advertisements, Indian women compete equally with Caucasian women in each of the beauty types under study and are being portrayed as elegant, decorative, cute, and even as sex kittens. Indian women's roles and appearances are becoming redefined, complementing their changed attitudes towards looking and feeling good and also treading the paths of independence and assertiveness. She finds there is limited exploitation of women's bodies as the portrayal of women in advertising is utilitarian, their beauty types and occupational roles chosen to fit the products being advertised. The author defines modern Indian women's stereotypes as independent, wearing a mix of Indian and Western clothes, being depicted as decision makers, and as a target for high-end services and goods. This new ideal, says Karan, is replacing the traditional stereotype of Indian women who were wearing mostly Indian clothes, promoting accessories and household products, and being shown in the traditional roles of mother or housewife.

In what almost amounted to a controlled experiment, Visnawanath and Balasubramanian studied the advertising imagery of women four years prior to and six years after the incursion of globalized business and advertising to India. In "Beauty and the Beast: Economic Liberalization, Advertising, and Construction of Beauty in Indian Advertising" they examine the forces of structural change and economic liberalization reflected by new international products entering the Indian market to explicate their impact on women in advertising. Starting in 1991, foreign companies were allowed to enter the Indian economy without surrendering majority shareholding. The ensuing flood has had an impact at many levels, but it is in the consumer market that it is most obvious. Whereas most countries experience globalization as a gradual process, the impact of globalization in India was far swifter as the transnational corporations fulfilled their pent-up desire to engage the Indian consumer. From 1991 onwards, what the global corporations had learned over the previous decades was applied with alacrity in India. The clear demarcation between before and after presented these authors with an unparalleled opportunity to study the changes that manifested in advertising.

The authors provide solid evidence of the ensuing makeover of women's images in Indian advertising. They found that the frequency of "thin" models appearing in women's magazine ads leaped ten-fold when they compared samples from 1987 and 1997. In addition, by 1997 the proportion of dark-skinned models dropped to a tenth of what it had been in 1987. As for cultural indicators, they found that the frequency of models wearing traditional Indian clothing fell by a third and that the appearance of traditional bangles and necklaces halved over the 10-year period.

Visnawanath and Balasubramanian caution us not to assume that changes in the way women are represented in ads reflect actual changes. Despite their expectation that urbanization, industrialization, and greater access to education would be reflected in increasing numbers of women taking up independent careers outside the home, they found that the incidence of women being shown in career roles in advertising actually fell by 25% over the ten years between their sampling years. One hopes that this illustrates the disconnect between actual reality and the constructed reality of advertising rather than a reversal in the trend of Indian women engaging in out-of-home employment.

WOMEN IN AN ISLAMIC CULTURE

In "Representation of Pakistani Women in the Media: Does Presence Mean Power?" Siddiqua Ovais brings to light the historical, political, traditional, and religious values and laws that influence the status and roles of women in Pakistan and notes that although the media continue to reflect and reinforce these norms, progress is being made.

Though they are hampered by traditions and laws that militate against their independence, Pakistani women are negotiating for space and autonomy, and organizing politically and socially to redefine the parameters of their existence. Government laws and regulations are changing to facilitate women entering the workplace, and at the same time, the media are beginning to reflect the increasing freedom of women and granting them more space. Television news anchors and readers can now appear in Western attire, whereas not long ago, women appearing on TV were required to cover their heads. These developments, argues Ovais, are an indication of a society becoming more tolerant and granting a greater visibility and voice to its women.

The author points out, however, that this liberalization is not yet reflected in the portrayal of women in advertising. The author, using content analysis of magazine advertisements, finds that although there is a shift in the social structures, the representation of women in advertising continues to reflect traditional stereotypes. Advertisements generally present the ideal Pakistani woman as meek, submissive, and contentedly confined to her home, caring for her family. These portrayals, says Ovais, perpetuate the conventional wisdom that women working outside the home results in extramarital affairs, the break up of families, and neglected children. Advertisements can often be useful indicators of current stereotypes, and in Pakistan, her analysis reveals, there is a disconnect between the actual, emerging roles of women and the stereotypical roles in which they are depicted.

CONCLUSION

This collection of studies on the content and context of images of Asian women in the commercial media provides some insight into the history, politics, economic policies, traditions, religious factors, and the laws and regulations that affect the representation of women in the media and advertising. They draw attention to the ways that the media persist in reflecting stereotypical images of women, but they also note that women in a number of countries use these images for empowerment.

In the context of understanding the changing roles and status of women in Asia we see that while they are becoming a powerful force, contributing to economic development, occupying and sometimes dominating major positions in diverse fields ranging from politics and administration to media and manufacturing, they are still often being shown in ads in less than powerful ways. In some countries, religious and deeply seated philosophical constraints affect women's status and the roles they play in advertising. On reflection, one could conclude that advertisers pay scant attention to the social conditions of women while they exploit them as consumers. However, on the whole, the chapters in this book reflect the changes that are gradual but noteworthy and should provoke some discussion on both the positive and negative reflections of women in Asian media.

REFERENCES

Bond, M. (1986). *The psychology of the Chinese people*. London: Oxford University Press.

Fung, A. (2000). Feminist philosophy and cultural representation in the Asian context. *Gazette: The International Journal of Communication Studies, 62*(2), 153-165.

2

HOLDING UP HALF OF THE "GROUND?"

Women Portrayed in Subway Advertisements in China

Hong Cheng

Guofang Wan

Since the Communists came to power in 1949, "Women hold up half of the sky" has been used as a "tagline" for both promoting and celebrating women's liberation in China. In this chapter, we give a twist to this persisting political slogan to highlight the nature and focus of our study.

Advertising came back to life in China in 1979 (Cheng, 1996, 2000; Xu, 1990). Each year since then, it has been growing at a phenomenal, double-digit rate. By 2003, advertising spending in China had reached 107.87 billion yuan (US$13.02 billion), a growth of 19.44% from the previous year (Wen, 2004), making China the second largest advertising market in Asia and the fifth largest in the world (Madden, 2004).

Although small in total billings when compared with other advertising genres, out-of-home advertising (including subway advertising) has been growing very fast in China and is becoming increasingly eye-catching. In 2002, out-of-home advertising billings in the country reached 9.99 billion yuan (US$1.21 billion), a 24.83% increase over the previous year (*China Advertising Yearbook*, 2003). In 2003, subway advertising experienced the fastest growth in comparison with other types of out-of-home advertising in China. Its share of the total out-of-home advertising billings increased to 8% from the 6% in 2002 (Chi, 2005). This growth is expected to continue as advertisers seek alternatives to the declining audiences and advertising clutter of other mass media forms.

Regarded as "the latest frontier for ads" (Ellison, 2001), the public spaces in subways of global cities such as Beijing and Shanghai have become very appealing to advertisers:

> Millions of commuters descend daily into the subway tunnels of Asia's global cities to stand on tiled platforms, waiting for the next train to arrive and accelerate them toward workplace and home. As they jostle to maintain balance in a herd of humanity, their eyes are drawn to wondrous scenes facing them across the tracks: beautiful faces, strong bodies, fantastic vistas, exotic animals, mouth-watering foods, glittering artifacts and shining machines. Like windows onto a consumer paradise, the brightly backlit, bed-sized subway advertisements beckon commuters to cross the tracks and climb into an imaginary life of luxury and comfort. (Lewis, 2003, p. 262)

A recent survey of 316 subway passengers and an observation of another 1,002 conducted by the Beijing-based *International Advertising* magazine and the International Advertising Institute indicated that 45.5% of passengers on platforms read the taglines and visuals of advertising posters in Beijing subways and 43.9% of them read the advertising content carefully while waiting for the train. Of the passengers surveyed, 71.2% of them reported that they even noticed when old advertisements were replaced with new ones in the subways. What was more, among the 119 brands advertised in Beijing subways, the passengers surveyed mentioned 72 of them (60.5%) without any hint (Li & Ma, 2005).

According to the same survey, 89.2% of the passengers taking Beijing subways were between 18 and 40 years old and had a university degree and a medium-level income. Most of these passengers took the subways on a regular basis, 32.2% of them daily, and 34.7% of them two to three times a week (Li & Ma, 2005). Apart from being young and educated, subway passengers in Beijing and Shanghai were "predominantly female" (Lewis, 2003, p. 262).

In spite of the rapid growth, proved attention, and perceived impact of subway advertising, little research has been done on this media class. Also of interest is the cultural content of this increasingly eye-catching advertising genre, which has saturated the public spaces in many global cities' subways (Lewis, 2003). Based on the growing importance of subway advertising and its potential influence on subway passengers, we believe that subway advertisements provide an ideal and significant platform for furthering the long-standing intellectual inquiries into women's images in advertising.

For decades, portrayals of women have been seen as an important indicator of codified behavior in all societies and as an effective way to examine advertising (Whipple & Courtney, 1985). Social-scientific studies have indicated that the portrayal of women in advertising, as an agent of socialization, exerts considerable influence on the thought patterns of society (Bardhan, 1995; Dyer, 1982). As a central issue in advertising, the portrayal of women was also found to affect directly the effectiveness of advertising campaigns, especially those targeting women.

As the portrayal of women has become an important issue of global advertising (Frith & Mueller, 2003), in this chapter we examine how women are currently portrayed in Chinese advertising, with a focus on subway advertising and with men as a meaningful point of comparison for our investigation. We hope that this study kills two birds with one stone—by examining the current status of women's portrayals in Chinese advertising, a fast-growing global advertising market, and by extending the scope of advertising research to subway advertising, a worthy but largely neglected genre.

Women's Role and Status in China

The People's Republic of China, with a total of 1.3 billion people, contains 20% of the world's population. Currently about 634 million women live in China, accounting for 48.8% of the nation's total population (CIA, 2005). In the traditional China that endured for several millennia, women's status was "little better than a slave's" (Curtin, 1975, p. 10). As Li (1988) noted, "Few societies in history have prescribed for women a more lowly status or treated them in a more routinely brutal way than traditional Confucian China" (p. 5). Discrimination against women was institutionalized within all the usual structures of society: family, the economy, education, culture, and the political system (Pearson, 1995). In China's age-old patriarchal and feudal conditions of society and culture, a person born female would be perceived by society to be in the lifelong position of *yin*. The *yin* position was the *kun* (earth, feminine) position. Far back in Chinese antiquity, *Yi Jing* (title in the U.S.: *I Ching*, or the *Book of Changes*)—the book of divination and sorcery—had already defined the attributes of this position: "*Kun* means *shun* (obedience, submission). *Shun* means "to obey" because of the "lowliness" of this position. In contrast to *yin*, perceived as the earth, lowly and inferior, is *yang*, seen as the sky, lofty and honored (Lin, 2000). This men-as-superior and women-as-inferior mentality was entrenched in China for thousands of years. Take the family for example: A woman in traditional China was shackled with feudal ethics called "the three obediences"; namely, obedience to her father before marriage, to her husband after marriage, and to her sons after the death of her husband (Su, 1996).

The binding of women's feet, introduced throughout China in the 10th century and seen as a mark of gentility for hundreds of years, was originally meant to restrain women when they went out of doors (Curtin, 1975).

Women were deprived of the right of self-determination in love affairs and marriage, and most marriages were arranged on a monetary basis. A Chinese woman's traditional role in life was to perpetuate the family name by bearing male children. If she did not fulfill this task, she could be cast out of her husband's home, disgraced, and socially ostracized (Su, 1996).

In the wake of the Democratic Revolution of 1911, women's status in China began to improve (Li, 1988). Later, millions of women participated in the Chinese Revolution, seeing in it the means for their emancipation. The decisive, fatal blow to the age-old forces that held Chinese women in subjugation, however, was the Communist victory in 1949 (Curtin, 1975). The All-China Women's Federation was established that year to help, among other things, reduce household responsibilities for working women and to educate women to adopt a "correct" attitude towards marriage, family, and the elderly (Li, 1988). In 1950, the Marriage Law of the People's Republic of China was passed to ensure the full freedom of marriage (Curtin, 1975). Chinese women have also gained the personal right to retain their maiden names. In cities, some children even take their mothers' surnames.

The most substantial post-1949 improvement in women's social status is that now nearly all young women are employed outside the home (Li, 1988). Women holding managerial positions are becoming more noticeable in China. Statistics show that 46% of businesses registered in China after 1995 are headed by women. Among these, 41% are privately owned. A recent survey also reported that Chinese businesswomen on average made more money than their male counterparts—especially those in the annual income bracket of 100,000 to 500,000 yuan (about US $12,000 to US $60,000), where women surpassed men by 5.2% ("Chinese Women Outshine," 2003).

Another major elevation of Chinese women's status has been through increased opportunities for school education. The illiteracy rate for women dropped from 90% in 1949 to less than 15% in 2002 (CIA, 2005). In 2002, 3.97 million female students were enrolled in China's higher institutions, or 43.95% of all university students in the country ("Female University Students Gaining on Men," 2003), an increase of more than five percentage points from the 38.31% in 1998. At the same time, "the proportions of girl students in different degrees also increased with the fastest growth rate for women doctors" ("Urban-Rural Gap," 2005). As a result of more women receiving formal education in China, the number of female professionals in science and technology and in higher education has increased significantly as well. In 2001, for example, there were 210,000 female full and associate professors in China's universities, counting for 40% of the total senior faculty in the universities of the country ("The Percentage of Females Receiving Higher Education," 2002).

Studies have also found, however, that problems still exist in China regarding women's rights and status. Pearson (1996) pointed out that a number of circumstances have combined during the period of reform to put women in an even more disadvantageous position now than at any other time since 1949. Many women workers in former state-owned and -operated enterprises have found themselves the first to be put out of work—as a result of economic restructuring and downsizing, but also on the grounds that a woman should not be regarded as the principal income-earner in a family (Goodman, 2002). Richards (1996) observed that China's one-child policy has been successful to a large extent but that it has raised new problems, citing female infanticide and the abortion of female fetuses, the disproportion of males over females in the population, the rise in the number of bachelors, and the abduction of women.

Studies have shown that more than two decades of reform in China "have considerably reduced the number and proportion of women serving in senior positions of political leadership" (Goodman, 2002, p. 332). There remain, as before, few female senior leaders of the Chinese Communist Party (CCP), ministers of the central government, or provincial leaders of the party-state. Although women continue to serve as deputy mayors in many Chinese cities and hold a number of ministerial appointments, and although every provincial leadership group has at least one mandatory woman member, their numbers remain low in government (Goodman, 2002).

Even some Chinese government media such as *China Daily* report that "despite the success stories of many individual women, the actual experience of far too many women, especially professional women, suggests that the promise of equality has not yet fully materialized" (Chang, 2004, p. 5). Some researchers in China have pointed out that Chinese women are today in the most difficult time since they were granted the same social and working status as men half a century ago. One dilemma is especially obvious and challenging to many young and educated women: Many professional women find themselves caught between career and family, tradition and modernity, and their actual ability and the social structure. Putting their own traditional roles as mothers and wives ahead of their roles as career women, many Chinese women are still not fully liberated. Among 17,860 people employed by research institutions in Shanghai, for example, 32.7% are women. However, only 15% of them have senior titles. And only 42% of 428 women scientists and researchers surveyed lead their own research projects. The survey also found that 82.9% of them had not been promoted in the previous five years. Among those lucky enough to have been promoted, most have only had one promotion (Chang, 2004).

Many people believe that even though women are entitled by the law to enjoy the same status and treatment as men, the traditional mindset regarding women has changed little: If a man is successful, it is considered normal for his wife to be responsible for the care of the family. This is seen as the ideal marital arrangement. If a woman is successful, however, she still needs to be a good wife and mother at home if she is to be regarded as a "good woman." Today still, unfortunately, many women in China share this mentality (Chang, 2004; "Men Want Career; Women Want Men," 2004).

In sum, it is evident that Chinese women's social and economic status has improved significantly over the past half a century. But it is also apparent that the age-old gender bias against women still remains strong in China, which constitutes a major barrier to women's full equality with men.

LITERATURE REVIEW AND RESEARCH HYPOTHESES

Content analysis, a major method for research on gender roles depicted in advertising, has been used for decades to document patterns in the portrayals of men and women (Cooper-Chen, Leung, & Cho, 1995). In fact, studies in this domain could be the subject of an article-length review in their own right. We review only those studies that we believe are the most relevant to our study in the following paragraphs.

Occupational and Family Roles

Opportunities for women to work outside home and their roles in families are two important indicators of women's social status in China. Over the past few decades, many researchers have paid great attention to occupation and family-related roles of women portrayed in advertising. As early as 1971, Courtney and Lockeretz reported that U.S. advertisements portrayed women as only having a place in the home, incapable of making important decisions, and fully dependent on men. Over the more than 30 years since then, many follow-up studies (Belkaoui & Belkaoui, 1976; Busby & Leichty, 1993; Cornelius, Thompson, Melanson, & Zelaya, 1996; Kerin, Lundstrom, & Sciglimpaglia, 1979; Lewis & Neville, 1995; Stohlton, 2003; Sullivan & O'Conner, 1988; Wagner & Banos, 1973) have also been largely devoted to women's working and family roles portrayed in U.S. magazine advertisements. Their conclusion was that stereotyping in the portrayal of women has continued over the decades, although the percentage of women shown as professionals and managers has made modest gains since the late 1950s (Cornelius et al., 1996).

In the late 1980s, many advertising researchers extended their attention to studies of women's occupation and family-related roles portrayed outside the United States. Gilly (1988) initiated such a study by comparing television commercials from Australia, Mexico, and the United States. She reported that women were likely to appear at home or outdoors and men were likely to be shown in occupational settings in U.S. commercials. Wiles and Tjernlund (1991) compared the portrayals of men and women in magazine advertisements from the United States and Sweden. They suggested that men were more often shown in work roles in U.S. advertisements and in non-work roles in Swedish advertisements.

Griffin and his collaborators (1994) found that U.S. advertisements contained a higher frequency of occupational roles whereas Indian advertisements had a stronger tendency to portray women performing duties in the home. Similarly, Bardhan (1995) reported that Indian women were depicted as putting their domestic obligations before the demands of their careers. In the same year, Sengupta reported in a study of women portrayals in U.S. and Japanese advertising that women appeared in working roles nearly twice as frequently in U.S. commercials as in Japanese ones. In a comparative study of sex roles in Japanese, Hong Kong, and Korean magazine advertisements, Cooper-Chen, Leung, and Cho (1995) found that, when portrayed in occupational roles, men prevailed over women in the "high-level business" and "professional" categories by about two to one.

In 1997, Cheng compared the gender roles portrayed in Chinese and U.S. television commercials. Results showed that advertising in both countries portrayed more men in occupational roles and more women in non-occupational ones. Chinese television advertising was found to reinforce even more stereotypes than its U.S. counterpart. For example, in Chinese commercials, male models played relaxing roles more often but family roles less often than female models.

Based on the previous studies of women's occupation- and family-related roles portrayed in advertising, the first two hypotheses for this study of the subway advertisements in China were formulated as follows:

H1: *Women are portrayed more often than men in non-occupational roles in Chinese subway advertisements.*

H2: *When portrayed in family settings, women in Chinese subway advertisements are shown more often than men in fulfilling family duties.*

Models' Dresses

As advertising has long been criticized for taking advantage of women's bodies in its promotion of products and services, some researchers have paid great attention to how the concept of women as sex objects was used as an attention grabber in advertisements (Choi & Leshner, 2003; Eagle, 1979; Ferguson, Kreshel, & Tinkham, 1990; Reichert & Carpenter, 2004; Soley &

Kurzbad, 1986; Venkatesan & Losco, 1975). Although most researchers mainly paid attention to women, some scholars focused on men's roles portrayed in U.S. magazine advertisements (Kolbe & Albanese, 1996; Skelly & Lundstrom, 1981; Wholheter & Lammers, 1980). They concluded that advertising tended to make much more frequent use of sexual displays of women's bodies than of men's. In 1994, Griffin and his collaborators reported that U.S. advertisements had a higher frequency of sexual body displays than did Indian advertisements.

When it comes to models' dresses, they can be roughly classified as either demure or seductive (Sengupta, 1995). Demure clothing, or everyday clothing, includes formal dress plus walking shorts, but excludes short-shorts and underwear. Seductive dress, on the other hand, includes clothing that partially exposes the upper body, such as unbuttoned blouses or muscle shirts. This category also includes very short shorts (Reichert & Carpenter, 2004; Soley & Reid, 1988). In 1997, Cheng reported that women tended to be portrayed more often in seductive dress than men although women were shown in demure dress more frequently in Chinese television commercials than in U.S. television commercials.

Frith, Cheng, and Shaw (2004) analyzed advertisements from women's fashion and beauty magazines in Singapore, Taiwan, and the United States. They compared the ways in which Western and Asian models were portrayed in print advertisements. They found that Western models were shown more frequently than Asian models in seductive dress. Based on those earlier studies, we formulated Hypotheses 3 and 4 for this study of women's portrayals in Chinese subway advertisements:

H3: *When it comes to the dress of models, women in Chinese subway advertisements are portrayed more often than men in seductive dress.*

H4: *When it comes to the dress of female models, Caucasian models in Chinese subway advertisements are portrayed more often in seductive dress than their Chinese counterparts.*

Product Categories

Several previous studies have reported that the portrayals of women were, to certain extent, related to the categories of the products being advertised. In their comparative study of Japanese, Hong Kong, and Korean magazine advertisements, Cooper-Chen, Leung, and Cho (1995) noticed that in Japan the product categories most strongly associated with women were cosmetics, but in Hong Kong and Korea women were associated most strongly with clothes. Men were most strongly associated with clothes in Hong Kong and Korea, but with entertainment/information in Japan. Similarly, Cheng (1997) found that gender-role portrayals in Chinese and U.S. television commercials also had much to do with the product categories advertised. While male models were most frequently used for food/non-alcohol beverage commercials in China, female models were most often used for home appliance commercials. As far as the entertainment/information product category was concerned, male models were used far more often than their female counterparts in both Chinese and U.S. television commercials.

Interestingly, Frith, Cheng, and Shaw (2004) found that Asian models were used more frequently in advertisements for hair and skin beauty products, whereas Western models dominated the clothing category. They pointed out that Western models were used more often than Asian models in body-oriented advertisements, and that Western models were used in advertisements in Asia when the underlying marketing strategy was that "sex sells." Although there seems to be no general agreement as to how gender portrayals relate to different ways product categories are advertised, we were able to posit a hypothesis that would allow us determine whether an observable pattern for such a relationship exists in Chinese subway advertisements.

H5: *There is a noticeable pattern for products advertised and genders portrayed in Chinese subway advertisements.*

DATA ANALYSIS

In this section, we relate how we collected and analyzed the data for this study of gender portrayals in Chinese subway advertisements.

Sample Collection

Today, six major metropolises in the Chinese mainland—Beijing, Shanghai, Tianjin, Nanjing, Guangzhou, and Shenzhen—have subway services (Schwandl, 2005). We selected Beijing and Shanghai subways for this study simply because they are the largest in the country (Schwandl, 2005) and because these two metropolises are among the leading advertising markets in China (Wen, 2004). Beijing Subway, which opened its first line to traffic in 1965, now has four lines in service, with a total length of 114 km (about 71 miles). It serves about 1.5 million passengers per day. With its first line opened in 1995, Shanghai currently has four subway lines, with a total length of 83 km (about 52 miles) serving a total of 1.22 million passengers per day (Schwandl, 2005).

We visited these two subway systems in mid-June 2003. As there were no major public or traditional holidays during that period, we believe the timing for this study allowed us to collect a sample that was representative of the typical advertisements posted in the subway systems. We randomly selected two of the four lines in each subway system, and we rode from one end to the other on all the four lines selected from these two cities. Having the four subway lines as our sampling universe, we alighted from the subway train at every third station and used digital cameras to take a picture of every other backlit, bed-sized advertising poster hanging on the tunnel wall facing the passenger platforms. We gathered a total of 1,158 advertising posters from the four selected Beijing and Shanghai subway lines.

Coding Instrument

Because our purpose was to examine the portrayals of women in Chinese subway advertisements in comparison with the portrayals of men, we removed those posters without adult female or male models from our database of samples. In addition, those advertisements only showing cartoon figures or crowd scenes where individuals were hard to see were excluded. Following the principle practiced by Gilly (1988), Sengupta (1995), and Cheng (1997), we retained duplicated advertisements for this study. Following Cooper-Chen, Leung, and Cho's (1995) coding strategy, we included partial figures for which gender was clear whenever at least part of the face was visible. The final pool consisted of 487 subway advertisements.

The coding scheme for this analysis was developed largely on the basis of previous studies on gender portrayals in advertising. We organized our product categories by following a scheme formulated by Venkatesan and Losco (1975). We based the occupational categories on those developed by Courtney and Lockeretz (1971). The dichotomy in the dress worn by models we borrowed from Sengupta (1995).

Coding Procedure

Male and female models in each advertisement were first coded into "occupational" and "non-occupational" roles. Then, "family" setting in the non-occupational roles was further coded into "family duties," which included cooking, cleaning, or childcare, and "relaxing," which referred to eating, sleeping, or watching television. The types of dress models wore in each subway advertisement were also coded. While those variables regarding models were coded, the product advertised in each advertisement was also classified.

A total of 487 subway advertisements showing adult males, females, or both males and females were coded independently by a pair of selected and trained coders fluent in both Chinese and English. The coders did not know the hypotheses for this study when conducting the coding. With a pre-test of 50 advertisements from the database, the code scheme was modified accordingly. When the coding was completed, we calculated a series of inter-judge reliabilities, using a per-item-agreement method suggested by Kassarjian (1977) and Stempel (1989). Ten percent of the advertisements were systematically selected and respectively recoded for all variables, which ranged from 88.7% to 100%. Each figure exceeded the minimum interjudge reliability of 85% recommended by Kassarjian (1977). We believe, therefore, that the coefficients of reliability we obtained are satisfactory. The consider-ably high coefficients of reliability here are understandable because of the simple nature of most variables in our analysis.

RESULTS

We summarize the results of our content analysis of the subway advertise-ments in China in Tables 2.1–2.6 (see Appendix). As shown in Table 2.1, 77.2% female models used in these advertisements were portrayed in "non-occupational" roles and only 22.8% of them were shown in "occupational" roles. In contrast, 60.8% of male models were depicted in "occupational" models, whereas only 39.2% of them were seen in "non-occupational" roles. These finding is statistically significant (X^2 = 69.547; $p < .001$; df = 1) and therefore supports Hypothesis 1. Also supporting Cheng's (1997) report on women's under-representation in Chinese television commercials, our cur-rent finding indicates that such an under-representation of women prevails in today's Chinese subway advertising.

When portrayed as playing "non-occupational" roles, for example in family settings, 71.1% women were found fulfilling family duties such as cooking, taking care of the children, or doing other house chores, whereas only 24.0% males were found involved in such family duties. On the con-trary, 76.0% men were found relaxing in family settings in comparison with only 28.9% women doing so (see Appendix, Table 2.2). This finding is sta-tistically significant (X^2 = 14.374; $p < .001$; df = 1) and therefore supports Hypothesis 2. This finding also supports Cheng's (1997) study on gender roles portrayed in family settings in Chinese television commercials. This finding indicates that many marketers still tend to portray Chinese men and women stereotypically in family settings, although in reality many husbands and wives share their family duties.

To demonstrate how advertisers use cues to suggest occupational roles, we include two of our photographs of the subway advertisement samples (see Figures 2.1 and 2.2). In the subway ad for Colgate (Figure 2.1) we see a man dressed in a dentist's outfit speaking to a young boy who appears to be his patient. Apparently the dentist is offering his patient some advice about how to take care of his teeth with the advertised product, Colgate. The "OK" gesture the dentist is using and the smile he is giving to the young boy compliment the boy on the excellent job he has done with the recommended toothpaste. The general impression of this advertisement is that the man, as a professional in dentistry, has the expertise and authority to offer tips to children and adults on how to take care of their teeth. He also serves as the spokesperson for the Chinese Medical Association and the Chinese Stomatological Association in their endorsement of the Colgate toothpaste (the two Chinese professional associations' endorsement was indicated by their logos at the right corner of the advertisement).

In the advertisement in Figure 2.2, we see a female model playing a mother's role in the family, doing the hair of a young girl model who acts as her daughter. The advertised product in this advertisement is ginseng, which root "has long been regarded by the Chinese as a panacea for illness, though it was usually used by them in a prophylactic (preventive) rather than a curative manner" (*Encyclopædia Britannica Online*, 2005). How is the mother-daughter image related to ginseng? The two vertical lines of Chinese text on the right of the advertisement bring out this connection: "From my childhood to adulthood, Mom's million threads of care are beyond words. This Chinese New Year, I'll take some *Wanji* (the brand name of the advised ginseng) home—to bring my best wishes to Dad and Mom for their good health." What a touching thought from the woman in the advertisement! Like her daughter, she used to sit on a chair and have her hair taken care of by her mother, who is now most likely getting old and needs some care from her in return.

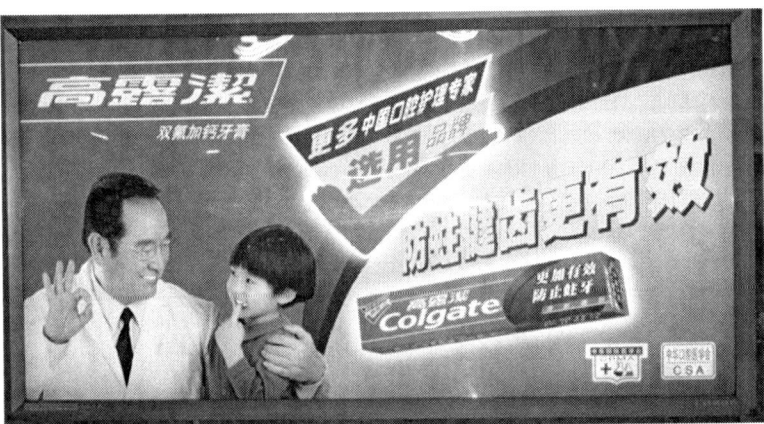

Figure 2.1. Photo by Hong Cheng and Guofang Wan

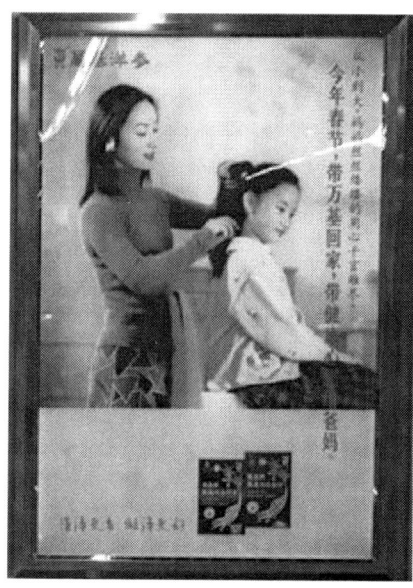

Figure 2.2. Photo by Hong Cheng and Guofang Wan

Although both advertisements have, coincidentally, a child in them and both adult models in the ads look happy and seem to be enjoying what they are doing, they are put in two different roles—an occupational role for the man and a traditional homemaker role for the woman. So, the male model relates to the child professionally, the female model maternally. These two ads illustrate our findings that women are portrayed more often than men in non-occupational roles in Chinese subway advertisements, and that when portrayed in family settings, women in Chinese subway advertisements are shown more often than men in fulfilling family duties.

The way advertising models are dressed is culturally symbolic and meaningful. As shown in Table 2.3 (Appendix), 59.5% of female models were dressed seductively when compared with the mere 7% of men that could be regarded so. By contrast, 95.9% of men were portrayed in demure clothing, but only 40.5% of women were depicted in a similar "serious" and "conservative" fashion. This finding is statistically significant (X^2 = 141.846; $p < .001$; df = 1) and therefore supports Hypothesis 3. This finding also supports Cheng's (1997) finding on how female models were dressed in Chinese television commercials. It indicates that many marketers in China still tend to use women's bodies to help promote and sell their products.

When looking at models' ethnic backgrounds, we found that 87.7% of Caucasian female models were dressed seductively, in comparison with only 19.6% of Chinese female models who could be seen that way (see Appendix, Table 2.4). This difference is also statistically significant (X^2 = 140.333; $p <$

.001; df = 1) and therefore supports Hypothesis 4. This finding strongly supports Frith, Cheng, and Shaw's (2004) report that Western models were shown more frequently than Asian models in seductive dress. In other words, Chinese subway advertising is strengthening the worldwide stereotypical view that Caucasian women tend to dress seductively; and these advertisements are reinforcing the misconception that it is okay to portray Caucasian women in this fashion.

We also found that male and female models tended to be used more often for certain product categories. Female models were used most often for cosmetics/personal care products (28.8%) and clothes (22.8%); male models were used most frequently for clothes (24.6%) and information/entertainment (21.1%) (see Table 2.5). This finding is statistically significant and thus supports Hypothesis 5. This finding also supports Cooper-Chen, Leung, and Cho's (1995) report that the products most strongly associated with women were cosmetics and clothes, and that men were most strongly associated with clothes and information/entertainment. This finding also supports Cheng's (1997) report that both Chinese and U.S. television commercials tended to use male models far more often than female models for the information/entertainment product category. This finding suggests that Chinese subway advertising is following an apparently global trend in advertising and tends to use male models more often in the promotion of new technology-related products and services (such as the Internet, laptop computers, and cellular phones).

Finally, we also found partial correlation between advertising models' race and their dress style. This partial correlation is directly related to product categories advertised. When product categories were uncontrolled, the partial correlation between advertising models' race and their dress style is .636 ($p < .01$). When product categories were controlled, however, this partial correlation reduced to .625 ($p < .001$) (see Table 2.6). The lowered coefficient after product categories were removed indicates that the correlation between advertising models' race and their dress style is partly due to the presence of product categories. This finding is consistent with Frith, Cheng, and Shaw's (2004) report that product categories did affect the correlations of some variables examined in advertising studies.

DISCUSSION AND CONCLUSION

Based on our findings, at least two points become evident: First, Chinese subway advertising mainly targets the perceived desires of young, predominantly female consumers, as it tends to portray women more often than men, and it tends to promote cosmetics/personal care products for women most often. These advertising strategies are by no means accidental. In fact, they could be many advertisers' deliberate efforts to follow the trends in today's rapidly rising Chinese consumerism. Since the initiation of its economic reforms in 1979, China has become one of the fastest growing economies in the world, emerging as a global economic force. In the past 10 years, more than 100 million people in China moved up to the middle class. Economists forecast that in another 10 years, China's middle class will be 400 million strong. A large portion of this affluent middle class is female (Frith, 2005).

As a combined influence of economic growth, educational opportunities, and technological development, women in China are becoming more assertive about their role in society nowadays than in the past. As one way of declaring themselves, young female consumers in major metropolises such as Beijing and Shanghai are particularly willing to pay top prices for imported beauty brands. These consumer trends indicate that subway advertisers in China, domestic and foreign alike, did the "right" thing by targeting young, predominantly female, consumers.

Nevertheless, "right" advertising strategies do not guarantee appropriate and effective advertising tactics or executions. This thought leads to our discussion of the second major finding of this study: In order to target heavily at young women, Chinese subway advertisers resort to many stereotypes commonly seen in advertising in other media classes in the country (Cheng, 1997) and in other countries (Cooper-Chen, Leung, & Cho, 1995; Frith, Cheng, & Shaw, 2004), such as the portrayals of women more often in non-occupational roles, in fulfilling family duties, and in a seductive dress style. These stereotypes in advertising executions may not be effective to the young, predominantly female, consumers in China at all; instead, they could offend many of the target consumers. According to a recent study conducted by Dove, one of Unilever's largest beauty brands, 64% of Chinese female respondents said the mass media and advertising tend to set unrealistic standards of beauty; nearly half of them (45%) thought the media and advertising portray women in clichéd ways; 59% of them criticized the models in beauty advertisements for not being good role models for young girls; and 67% of them wished the media could give women more confidence in their looks and beauty (Etcoff, Orbach, Scott, & D'Agostini, 2004).

These documented public opinions of female consumers in China clearly indicate that it is high time advertisers, including subway advertisers, in China began to "think out of the box," by creating executions that will be more relevant and more appropriate to their targeted young female urban consumers. Only by so doing can subway advertising be really effective to its target market. At least, the subway advertisers cannot afford to forget that it is only because those young female consumers they intend to reach with their advertising messages need to commute to *work* that they are exposed to the advertising in the subway.

According to the Integrated Marketing Communication (IMC) theory, each encounter a brand or its company has with its customers and even the general public, among others, should be constructive (Schultz, 2002). Any negative encounter may hurt the image of the brand and company, and eventually the sales of the company. So, in the short term, subway advertisers should consider the effectiveness of its messages by having not only "right" strategies but also "right" executions; in the long term, they should keep the images of their brands and companies, and social responsibility in mind. No matter in the short or long term, they should try to avoid any possible perceived negativity from their target consumers and the general public about their advertisements.

In sum, as China becomes more and more involved in modernization, urbanization, and globalization, the rapid growth of subway advertising makes it a media class worthy of exploration by advertising professionals as well as researchers. Chinese subway advertising is emulating current international trends in advertising gender portrayal. Advertising professionals should become more alert to the potential sociocultural impact; they should select both advertising strategies and executions more carefully to suit the needs of their target markets.

APPENDIX

Table 2.1
Gender-Role Portrayals by Sex

ROLES	MALES		FEMALES	
	n	(%)	*n*	(%)
Occupational	104	(60.8)	72	(22.8)
Non-occupational	67	(39.2)	244	(77.2)
Total	171	(100.0)	316	(100.0)

$X^2 = 69.547$; $p < .001$; df = 1

Table 2.2
Models' Roles in Family by Sex

ROLES	MALES		FEMALES	
	n	(%)	*n*	(%)
Family Duties	6	(24.0)	32	(71.1)
Relaxing	19	(76.0)	13	(28.9)
Total	25	(100.0)	45	(100.0)

$X^2 = 14.374$; $p < .001$; df = 1

Table 2.3
Models' Dress by Sex

DRESS	MALES		FEMALES	
	n	(%)	*n*	(%)
Demure	164	(95.9)	128	(40.5)
Seductive	7	(4.1)	188	(59.5)
Total	171	(100.0)	316	(100.0)

$X^2 = 141.846$; $p < .001$; df = 1

Table 2.4
Female Models' Dress by Race

DRESS	CHINESE		CAUCASIAN	
	n	(%)	n	(%)
Demure	152	(80.4)	16	(12.3)
Seductive	37	(19.6)	111	(87.7)
Total	189	(100.0)	127	(100.0)

$X^2 = 140.333$; $p < .001$; df = 1

Table 2.5
Models Used for Product Categories by Sex

PRODUCT CATEGORIES	MALES		FEMALES	
	n	(%)	n	(%)
Food/Non-alcohol	24	(14.0)	48	(15.2)
Clothes	42	(24.6)	72	(22.8)
Cosmetics/Personal Care	6	(3.5)	91	(28.8)
Drugs	20	(11.7)	18	(5.7)
Home Appliances	19	(11.1)	27	(8.5)
Information/Entertainment	36	(21.1)	48	(15.2)
Automobiles	6	(3.5)	0	(0.0)
Miscellaneous	18	(10.5)	12	(3.8)
Total	171	(100.0)	316	(100.0)

$X^2 = 63.222$; $p < .001$; df = 7

Table 2.6
Partial Correlation Between Models' Race and Dress

	RACE	
Dress	Uncontrolled*	Controlled**
	.636***	.625****

*Product categories are not partialled out.
**Product categories are partialled out.
***$p < .01$
****$p < .001$

REFERENCES

Bardhan, N. R. (1995). *Portrayal of women in the advertisements in India today—India's leading current affairs magazines: 1984–1994.* Paper presented at the AEJMC Annual Convention, Washington, DC.

Belkaoui, A., & Belkaoui, J. J. (1976). A comparative analysis of the roles portrayed by women in print advertisements, 1958, 1970, 1972. *Journal of Marketing Research, 13,* 168–172.

Busby, L. J., & Leichty, G. (1993). Feminism and advertising in traditional and non-traditional women's magazines 1950s–1980s. *Journalism Quarterly, 70,* 247–264.

Chang, T. (2004, October 2). Gender stereotypes still hold hamper female professionals. *China Daily,* p. 5.

Cheng, H. (1996). Advertising in China: A socialist experiment. In K. T. Frith (Ed.), *Advertising in Asia: Communication, culture and consumption* (pp. 73–102). Ames: Iowa State University.

Cheng, H. (1997). "Holding up half of the sky"? A sociocultural comparison of gender-role portrayals in Chinese and U.S. advertising. *International Journal of Advertising, 16,* 295–319.

Cheng, H. (2000). China: Advertising yesterday and today. In J. P. Jones (Ed.), *International advertising: Realities and myths* (pp. 255–284). Thousand Oaks, CA: Sage.

Chi, G. (2005). *An overview of China's out-of-home advertising in 2003.* Retrieved July 11, 2005, from http://www.emkt.com.cn/article/154/15499.html.

China Advertising Yearbook. (2003). An overview of China's advertising growth in 2002 (pp. 21–22). Beijing: Xinhua Publishing House.

Chinese women outshine the men in business. (2003, August 23). *The Straits Times,* p. 5.

Choi, Y. H., & Leshner, G. (2003). *Who are the "Others"? Third-person effects of idealized body image in magazine advertisements.* Paper presented at the 2003 AEJMC Annual Convention, Kansas City, MO.

CIA. (2005). "China." *The world factbook.* Retrieved July 10, 2005, from http://www.cia.gov/cia/publications/factbook/geos/ch.html#People.

Cooper-Chen, A., Leung, E., & Cho, S. H. (1995). Sex roles in East Asian magazine advertising. *Gazette, 55,* 207–223.

Cornelius, D., Thompson, C., Melanson, W., & Zelaya, C. (1996). *The portrayal of women in magazine advertising: A content analytical and comparative study.* Paper presented at the AEJMC Annual Convention, Anaheim, CA.

Courtney, A. E., & Lockeretz, S. W. (1971). A woman's place: An analysis of the roles portrayed by women in magazine advertisements. *Journal of Marketing Research, 8,* 92–95.

Curtin, K. (1975). *Women in China.* New York and Toronto: Pathfinder Press.

Dyer, G. (1982). *Advertising as communication.* London and New York: Methuen.

Eagle, J. (1979). The bad, the bare, and the beautiful. *Media Scope, 13,* 39.

Ellison, S. (2001, January 12–14). Subway tunnels are latest frontier for ads: New technology projects movie images on walls for riders to see. *The Asian Wall Street Journal,* p. 3.

Encyclopædia Britannica Online. (2005). Retrieved July 10, 2005, from http://search.
eb.com/eb/article?tocId=9036873&query=ginseng&ct=

Etcoff, N., Orbach, S., Scott, J., & D'Agostino, H. (2004, September). The real truth
about beauty: A global report [White paper commissioned by Dove, a Division
of Unilever]. Retrieved February 12, 2006, from http://www.campaignforreal-
beauty.com/uploadedfiles/dove_white_paper_final.pdf

Female university students gaining on men. (2003). *Xinhua News Agency.* Retrieved
July 10, 2005, from http://service.china.org.cn/link/wcm/Show_Text?info_id=
?72413 & pqry=?women%20and%20in%20and%20universities.

Ferguson, J. H., Kreshel, P. J., & Tinkham, S. F. (1990). In the pages of Ms.: Sex role
portrayals of women in advertising. *Journal of Advertising, 19,* 40–51.

Frith, K. T. (2005). *The rising dragon: Chinese consumerism.* Paper presented at the
13th International Conference on Advertising and Public Relations: Future
Trends and Developments in the Chinese Consumer Market, National
Chengchi University, Taipei, Taiwan.

Frith, K. T., & Mueller, B. (2003). *Advertising and societies: Global issues.* New York:
Peter Lang.

Frith, K. T., Cheng, H., & Shaw P. (2004). Race and beauty: A comparison of Asian
and Western models in women's magazine advertisements. *Sex Roles, 50,* 53–61.

Gilly, M. C. (1988). Sex roles in advertising: A comparison of television advertisements in Australia, Mexico, and the United States. *Journal of Marketing, 52,*
75–85.

Goodman, D. S. G. (2002). Why women count: Chinese women and the leadership
of reform. *Asian Studies Review, 26,* 331–353.

Griffin, M., Viswanath, K., & Schwarts, D. (1994). Gender advertising in the United
States and India: Exporting cultural stereotypes. *Media, Culture and Society, 16,*
487–507.

Kassarjian, H. H. (1977). Content analysis in consumer research. *Journal of
Consumer Research, 4,* 8–18.

Kerin, R. A., Lundstrom, W. J., & Sciglimpaglia, D. (1979). Women in advertisements: Retrospect and prospect. *Journal of Advertising, 8,* 37–42.

Kolbe, R. H., & Albanese, P. J. (1996). Man to man: A content analysis of sole-male
images in male-audience magazines. *Journal of Advertising, 25,* 1–20.

Lewis, C., & Neville, J. (1995). Images of Rosie—A content analysis of women
workers in American magazine advertising, 1940–1946. *Journalism and Mass
Communication Quarterly, 72,* 216–227.

Lewis, S.W. (2003). The media of new public spaces in global cities: Subway advertising in Beijing, Hong Kong, Shanghai, and Taipei. *Continuum: Journal of
Media and Cultural Studies, 17,* 262–272.

Li, C. Y. (1988). *The social status of women in China.* Unpublished MA thesis,
Department of Sociology, Southern Illinois University at Edwardsville.

Li, D. D., & Ma, F. (2005). A survey on the effectiveness of subway ads in Beijing.
Retrieved, July 10, 2005, from http://www.a.com.cn/cn/scdc/000816dtad.htm.

Lin, D. (2000). Chinese women's culture: From tradition to modernization. *Chinese
Education and Society, 33,* 24-36.

Madden, N. (2004, August 16). Two Chinas: Marketers face challenges of polarized
wealth and ethnic diversity. *Advertising Age, 1,* 22–23.

Men want career; women want men. (2004). *China Daily*. Retrieved July 10, 2005, from http://service.china.org.cn/link/wcm/Show_Text?info_id=?113089&p_qry=?women%20and%20in%20and%20universities.

Pearson, V. (1995). Goods on which one loses—women and mental health in China. *Social Science and Medicine, 41*, 1159–1173.

Pearson, V. (1996). Women and health in China. *Journal of Social Policy, 25*, 529–543.

The percentage of females receiving higher education is increasing in China. (2002). *China.com.cn*. Retrieved July 10, 2005, from http://www.china.org. cn/chinese/EDU-c/116358.htm.

Reichert, T., & Carpenter, C. (2004). An update on sex in magazine advertising: 1983 to 2003. *Journalism and Mass Communication Quarterly, 81*, 823-837.

Richards, L. (1996). Controlling China's baby boom. *Contemporary Review, 268*, 5–9.

Schultz, D. E. (2002). The next generation of integrated marketing communication. *Interactive Marketing, 4*, 318–319.

Schwandl, R. (2005). *UrbanRail.Net*. Retrieved July 10, 2005, from http://www.urbanrail.net/as/asia.htm.

Sengupta, S. (1995). The influence of culture on portrayals of women in television commercials: A comparison between the United States and Japan. *International Journal of Advertising, 14*, 314–333.

Skelly, G. U., & Lundstrom, W. J. (1981). Male sex roles in magazine advertising, 1959–1979. *Journal of Communication, 31*, 52–57.

Soley, L., & Kurzbard, G. (1986). Sex in advertising: A comparison of 1964 and 1984 magazine advertisements. *Journal of Advertising, 15*, 46–54.

Soley, L. C., & Reid, L. N. (1988). Taking it off: Are models in magazine ads wearing less? *Journalism Quarterly, 65*, 960–966.

Stempel III, G. H. (1989). Content analysis. In G. H. Stempel III & B. H. Westley (Eds.), *Research methods in mass communication* (2nd ed., pp. 124–136). Englewood Cliffs, NJ: Prentice Hall.

Stohlton, E. (2003). *The portrayal of men, women and children in* Parents Magazine *advertisements: 2000 and 2003*. Paper presented at the AEJMC Annual Convention, Kansas City, MO.

Su, B. (1996, March 11). Women's marital status: Past and present. *Beijing Review*, pp. 18–19.

Sullivan, G. L., & O'Conner, P. J. (1988). Women's role portrayals in magazine advertising: 1958–1983. *Sex Roles, 18*, 181–188.

Urban-rural gap in higher education narrows in China. (2005). *People's Daily Online*. Retrieved July 10, 2005, from http://english.people.com.cn/200502/16/eng20050216_173725.html.

Venkatesan, M., & Losco J. (1975). Women in magazine advertisements. *Journal of Advertising Research, 15*, 49–54.

Wagner, L. C., & Banos J. B. (1973). A woman's place: A follow-up analysis of the roles portrayed by women in magazine advertisements. *Journal of Marketing Research, 10*, 213–214.

Wen, G. (2004). Statistics and analysis of China ad market in 2003. *Modern Advertising, 4*, 36–38.

Whipple, T. W., & Courtney A. E. (1985). Female role portrayals in advertising and communication effectiveness: A review. *Journal of Advertising, 14*, 4–8, 17.

Wholheter, M., & Lammers H. B. (1980). An analysis of male roles in print adver-
    tisements over a 20-year span: 1958–78. In J. C. Olson (Ed.), *Advances in con-
    sumer research* (pp. 760–761). Ann Arbor, MI: Association for Consumer
    Research,

Wiles, C. R., & Tjernlund, A. (1991). A comparison of role portrayal of men and
    women in magazine advertising in the U.S.A. and Sweden. *International Journal
    of Advertising, 10,* 259–267.

Xu, B. (1990). *Marketing to China: One billion new consumers.* Lincolnwood, IL:
    NTC Business Books.

3

BEING A "GOOD" WOMAN
IN KOREA

The Construction of Female Beauty and Success

Kwangmi K. Kim

Heewon Cha

South Korea is in transformation from a traditional society into a more modern, "open," and Westernized society. Through its rapid economic growth and the rise of the middle class in recent decades, Korea has enjoyed the status and consumer buying power as one of Asia's "newly industrialized countries." At the same time, though, Korean society is embroiled in a continuing sociocultural tug-of-war between Confucianism and postmodernism—these conflicting ideologies coexisting in various aspects of Korean society. Traditional values such as collectivist, humanitarian, and authoritative stand in opposition to modern, individualist, materialist, and egalitarian values. Reconciling these opposites poses a challenge to a rapidly transforming society (Choy, 2000). In this chapter, we examine whether this ongoing transformation is being reflected in women's images depicted in leading Korean magazine advertisements. We focus on the construction of beauty, sex roles, and power relationships between men and women by examining dominant or idealistic images of women represented in magazine ads.

As a socializing agent and institution, the media have a powerful impact on our attitudes, values, beliefs, and behaviors, because all visual images, as nonverbal symbols, contribute to meanings and associations occurring in social interactions. The images conveyed by advertising have become so sophisticated and persuasive that they organize our experiences and understanding in a significant way. Several media scholars (Ewen & Ewen, 1992; Goldman, 1992; Kilbourne, 2000) have emphasized advertising's role as a major agent of social reinforcement due to its presumed power for molding opinions, attitudes, and behaviors. Therefore, advertising does not just sell us products and services but it also indirectly and subtly tells us ways to understand and to perceive the world. In other words, advertising becomes an important social, cultural, and economic institution, which strives to maintain cultural hegemony and the status quo by providing certain ways of seeing and making sense of our world.

Based on a study of the literature and using Goffman's (1979) categories for decoding behavior along with several other variables, we address the following questions:

1. Which gender behavior patterns have been the most prevalent in women's magazines in Korea? We analyze several important variables such as beauty type, gaze, product category, and the race of models.
2. What social messages do these magazine ads provide to Korean women in their 20s, 30s, and 40s? How do these images affect self-images of Korean women in general?
3. Have any legal and regulatory measures been positively reflected in the representation of female images in the media?
4. Is the representation of women in Korean magazine advertisements typical of international gender stereotypes? Considering the status of the Korean society as a dynamic and revolving society, what is the meaning of Western beauty in Korea as represented in magazine ads?

In conclusion, we discuss our findings in the context of the debate over whether media or advertisements simply reflect society or create a constructed reality.

TRANSFORMING SOCIETY: FROM TRADITION TO WHERE?

Several economic studies have noted that Korean women (particularly young, lower-class women) have made an enormous contribution to the nation's economic development through their cheap and prolonged labor in the 1970s, 1980s, and through the 1990s. Despite their extensive contribution to this remarkable economic development, the status of women in the economic and political arenas has been far from rewarding (Palley, 1990;

Park, 1993; Soh, 1993). Many people blame Korea's traditional value systems and social structures for the continuing low status accorded to women.

Basing them on Confucian philosophy, Korea has long maintained rigid gender roles that divided social life into the male/public and female/domestic spheres. In the domestic arena, the relationship between a husband and a wife has its basis in the Confucian ideology of male superiority that is rooted in the idea of yin/yang complementarities: The husband was metaphorically referred to as "heaven," to signify his superiority, and the wife (as "earth") was supposed to serve him with reverence. Traditionally, Korean people say that all women should follow the "three rules of obedience" over the course of their lives: obedience to father in childhood, to husband after marriage, and to son in her old age (Kim, 1979).

Within the Korean patriarchal tradition, however, strict gender-role specialization has accorded a great deal of autonomy and power to women in their own sphere. It sounds contradictory, but as women age—especially as mothers of successful sons—they earn increasing power and respect in their family and social life. Traditionally, having raised a successful family a woman is considered to have fulfilled her duty and calling as a mother and a wife.

Recent economic growth and development, however, is challenging traditional values and sociocultural behaviors. Women's attitudes towards their own place in family and society have been changing toward more positive and active roles, and women are seeing their relationship with men more as equal partnerships. Meanwhile, men's attitudes about women's roles have been changing more slowly. We have also witnessed some changes in government policy and laws affecting the status and interests of women in both domestic and public spheres (e.g., the Family Law and the Equal Opportunity Law). According to one nationwide survey (Park, 1993), only 5% of men were against women's employment. This survey shows that Korean society has become more accepting of women's social enhancement and is becoming more open to gender equality.

Even if a materialist culture has replaced some traditional values and lifestyles, traditional family values and gender relationships remain very central to most Koreans: Male superiority embedded in Confucianism is still alive in people's belief systems. Korea has one of the world's highest preferences for male births, and the majority of men are in favor of women working only after their children become independent adults (Park, 1993). In other words, conflicting modern and traditional values coexist, making women's roles much more complicated and precarious. Due to this complexity and the dynamic nature of the changes, Soh (1993) termed the transforming Korean society a "patriarchal democracy" (p. 74). She argued that Korean women and men tend to organize their everyday life by compartmentalizing the arena of social action—not only into public versus private spheres but also into formal versus informal situations within each sphere—and to negotiate egalitarian and traditional sexist attitudes in accordance with changing circumstances.

Intergenerational conflict adds another layer of complexity to the transforming Korean society. The consumption habits, values, and physical appearance of younger generations (mostly in their 20s and 30s) have undergone significant changes. Such changes are often attributed to increasing foreign influence through the overall globalization of society, the role of the media in particular, and through increased overseas travel. For example, attention to physical appearance and beauty became pervasive among Korean adults in their 20s and 30s. According to a survey by an advertising agency, 63% of single females and 46% of males responded that maintaining good body figure is the major priority in their daily lives (Daehong, 1999). As a result, they are willing to spend a fortune on plastic surgery for a better physical appearance. Increasingly, they are having their noses lifted, their jaws shaved, and their eyes widened in a drive to attain the Western image of beauty. More recently, young Korean women are having plastic surgery done on their calves in the hope of attaining the "Barbie" legs sported by the world's supermodels (Schuman, 2001). The plastic surgery business has become very lucrative—especially in Kangnam, the most affluent, upper-middle-class area of Seoul.

SELF-REGULATION OF PRINT ADVERTISING

The Korean Advertising Review Board, the country's self-regulatory body, was established in 1991 by eight advertising-related organizations (including the Korea Advertisers Association, the Korea Association of Advertising Agencies, and the Korea Newspapers Advertising Association) to bring advertising practices into line with social norms, to enhance the level of self-regulation, and to direct voluntary efforts towards increasing the trustworthiness of advertising. This board monitors advertisements published in 62 dailies, 50 magazines, and 103 special newspapers, and it refers "problematic" ads to the Advertising Deliberation Committee for decisions. This committee can take several actions depending on the degree of deviation found in the content and representation: caution, warning, correction, stopping, or requiring an apology advertisement. The Korea Advertising Review Board publishes their findings on advertising cases in their monthly magazine *Advertising Deliberation* (Korean Advertising Review Board, 2004a).

Self-regulatory guidelines contain 30 articles as general rules and another 22 articles as sectoral rules for specific areas such as food, tobacco, medicine and healthcare products, and cosmetics to enhance credibility and social responsibility of advertising. Three out of the 52 articles specifically relate to the representation of women:

Article 6, on human respect, states that advertisements should respect the dignity of all persons, and should not hurt or ridicule the reputation of foreign cultures or other ethnic groups.

Article 8, on dignity, specifies that all advertisements should be prepared with a sense of responsibility to consumers and to society. Article 8 lists five specific guidelines:

1. Advertisements should not violate public safety and social norms and ethics.
2. Advertisements should not condone violence or antisocial behavior.
3. Advertisements should not cause fear or distress.
4. Advertisements should not ridicule or exploit any physical disability or weakness.
5. Advertisements should contain nothing that is likely to cause grave or widespread offense or create a sense of inferiority.

Article 18 is about sexuality and presents three specific guidelines:

1. Advertisements should avoid the inappropriate use or exploitation of sexuality and the use of coarseness and undesirable innuendo.
2. Advertisements should not depict sex crimes such as rape and should not justify or ridicule these images.
3. Advertisements should not use any indecent images or copy that might provoke sexual desires, particularly in the media targeted to teenagers or mass audiences. (Korean Advertising Review Board, 2004b)

Although the Korean advertising guidelines do contain articles on sexuality, dignity, and maintaining social norms, they are not specific enough to address the equal treatment or representation of both genders. For example, the Code of Advertising Standards for Ireland has an article on decency and propriety, which states:

> Advertisements should respect the principle of the equality of men and women. They should avoid sex stereotyping and any exploitation or demeaning of men and women. Where appropriate, advertisements should use generic terms that include both the masculine and feminine gender; for example, the term "business executive" covers both men and women. (McGough, 2002, Ch. 7: 2.15)

The Korean advertising industry might consider reviewing the much stronger and specific guidelines from countries such as Ireland and Canada, and revising its own guidelines to match the changing social and cultural environment of Korean society.

LITERATURE REVIEW

Several studies have documented the impact of advertising on defining socially acceptable attitudes and behaviors. These studies have taken findings from different forms of media and concluded that "appropriate" gender behaviors for men and women in the United States have been delivered to the audience either in latent or manifest images. Findings have indicated that U.S. advertising not only reflects sex inequality in the workplace, but it reinforces and validates that inequality as well. Generally speaking, these findings can be summarized by the following stereotypes of women: as dependent on or subservient to men, as to be seen primarily at home or in domestic settings, as preoccupied with physical attractiveness, as sex objects and decorations for men, and as product users or demonstrators rather than as authority figures. Another typical image of women was as dependent, unintelligent consumers who were concerned with the social consequences of purchasing a product, whereas men tended to be portrayed as independent, intelligent, objective decision makers who demonstrated expertise and authority (Furnham & Skae, 1997).

Another stereotypical image of women in advertising relates to female sexuality. In the analysis of body positioning and facial expressions of female models in magazines, Rudman and Verdi (1993) revealed an illusion of reality in which females are flawless beauties who have been dehumanized and are passive and submissive to the whims of their male counterparts. On the other hand, males are portrayed as nondimensional in terms of being unemotional, aggressive, and needing to control the female. Female models are much more likely than male models to be portrayed in submissive roles. Krassas, Blauwkamp, and Wesselink (2001) adopted their classification of coding female images from Goffman (1979) and examined how certain poses transmit messages about the appropriate roles, looks, or behaviors for men and women. Using four *Playboy* and four *Cosmopolitan* magazines, they revealed that each magazine, although addressing different audiences, converges on a single construction of sexuality for women—dependency, submissiveness, and sexual availability.

Similarly, stereotypical images of males have appeared in magazine advertisements. Kolbe and Albanese (1996) looked at the camera angle of male models in 1993 issues of *Business Week, Sports Illustrated, Esquire,*

GQ, Rolling Stone, and *Playboy*. Their study revealed the media's idealistic world of male icons, such as the Marlboro Man cowboy image. According to them, "cowboy" is the quintessential image of the American male because it has all the traits of the ideal male: individualistic, insensible, cold, and implacable (p. 4).

Since the 1960s, feminists and other media critics have raised their voices and expressed strong concerns about the stereotypical portrayal of women and have brought the attention of both advertisers and the public to the manner in which the mass media depict females. This campaign against "perceived negative female images" by members of the National Organization of Women (NOW) and other women's groups objected to a Korean advertising industry that persists in reinforcing the "woman's place is in the home" attitude and portrays women as sexual objects. Interestingly, despite these efforts, stereotypical portrayals in advertising have not only continued, but have in some ways actually increased from the 1970s to the 1990s (Busby, 1975; Ferguson, Kreshal, & Tinkham, 1990; Ford et al., 1998; Gilly, 1988; Reichert et al., 1999).

These and similar studies are extremely important because one out of every four teenage girls in the United States suffers from an eating disorder, and some evidence exists for the prevalence of this condition increasing in societies influenced by social globalization. Teenage girls—and all women in fact—are daily confronted with a barrage of images depicting and glamorizing thin women. The media in general seem to be obsessed by the idea that thin equals beautiful. This continuous, limited representation of women in the media has been blamed for causing eating disorders, excessive dieting, and lack of self-esteem.

Depictions of stereotypical female roles tend to be universal phenomena: they appear in media throughout the world. Furnham, Abramsky, and Gunter (1997) argued that the gender stereotyping embedded in the U.S. media has been replicated in other countries such as Australia, Britain, Canada, and Italy. They claimed that although certain national idiosyncrasies have emerged, the broad pattern of gender portrayal on television advertising has crossed national boundaries. In a four-day workshop, "Changing the Images of Women in Media," held in Malaysia in 1990, participants from the Asia-Pacific region noted that women were typically portrayed in domestic, seductive, and subservient roles. They also pointed out that such images have perpetuated the idea of women as property or as commodities available for sexual and other use (Asia & Pacific: Strategies, 1990). Ford et al. (1998) examined popular Japanese magazines ads through content analysis and discovered that women were still being portrayed as more preoccupied with physical appearance, were being represented as younger than the men, and were not being depicted as product authorities. However, interestingly enough, this study also revealed that although stereotypical male images still dominate, some alternative images of men—devoted, obliging, rattle-brained (confused), and thorough—have appeared in recent ads. Until recently, these traits have been ascribed to women in advertisements.

Furnham, Mak, and Tanidjojo (2000) compared gender-role stereotypes in Hong Kong and Indonesia by analyzing their television commercials. They assumed that due to differences in these two countries (Hong Kong is more urban and modern than the Muslim Indonesia), gender-role stereotyping would be less apparent in Hong Kong television advertisements than in those found in Indonesian counterparts. However, they did not find any significant differences in gender-role stereotyping between the two countries, and rather concluded that this is a pan-Asian phenomenon. Furthermore, by comparing their study with similar ones conducted in Europe, they revealed that gender-role stereotyping, at least in television advertisements, is stronger in parts of the East Asia than in Europe.

Korean researchers have documented similar findings: Song (1991) analyzed the images of women portrayed in both women's and men's magazines and found that the core image of female models has remained consistent in both types of magazine. The typical image of women as sexual beings still dominated, and any change in the role of women in Korean society is not being reflected in advertising. In her analysis of four major women's magazines, Kim (1994) also revealed that the traditional women's roles as homemaker and mother have been leading images in the three decades since the 1970s. However, she also noted that magazine ads during the 1980s began to present more diverse women's roles, and in the 1990s presented nontraditional women's portrayals, such as in professional roles. Han (2002) presented similar findings in her analysis of television commercials. First, she found that female models have been most closely associated with products such as clothing, cosmetics, and detergents, whereas male models were used for more complex and expensive products such as computers, automobiles, and other machines. Second, she found that elegant, passive, and slim female models were presented as the ideal female image in the commercials and were shown caring for men or family members while remaining subservient to men.

Research is showing that women's images, as portrayed in the Korean media since 1994, have been slowly improving with the gradual appearance of positive and active roles for women. Chung's study (1997) of women's images of television commercials revealed that about 25% of ads showed a domestic homemaker image, another 25% contained female images with some body showing, 13.5% showed decorative images of women as sexual objects, and another 13.5% featured images of strong and independent women. Images of independent and active women have been on the increase, but traditional, stereotypical women's images still predominate. Another interesting finding in Chung's study was that when female models are portrayed with male models in the ads, the women's roles have been shifting toward the more stereotypical and traditional. When both genders appeared in the ads, domestic homemaker-type images dominated; decorative sexual roles have increased, while independent women's images have decreased. In addition, when shown at all, the occupation of female models was not very clear. This slight improvement in the portrayal of women in ads noted by Chung was confirmed by Han's (2002) study of the changes in masculine and feminine images depicted on TV commercials over the seven years from 1993 to 1999. Elegant and beautiful women's images were the most frequent, trailed by images of modernized and independent women.

This does not mean, though, that the representation of women in Korean advertising has been completely transformed into positive, diverse roles. Women's images are also limited in the sense that professional images still emphasize physical beauty. Regardless of the occupation or role portrayed, physical appearance and beauty have become the most prevalent attributes of women depicted in advertisements. The emphasis on women's beauty in ads remained constant throughout the seven-year period studied.

Studies of the representation of women in Asia-Pacific-region media illustrate some dilemmas. Whereas Asian societies have rapidly developed and expanded into modern industrial economies, social and cultural values have been slow to catch up. Traditional values are being inserted into mainstream commercial messages, and this accounts for the continued stereotypical and unequal representation of females in the media (Fung, 2000).

METHODS

We took a qualitative, historical approach in addressing our research questions. In addition, we used a small-scale quantitative analysis to dimension and further describe the dominant female images represented in the magazine advertisements.

The unit of analysis for this study was a full-page magazine advertisement containing a shoulders-up shot of one or more female models. In each qualifying ad, the face and part of the body had to be visible. Advertisements that featured female models were collected from popular Korean women's magazines published during 2002. As a convenience sample, three major popular women's magazines (*Women Sense, Lady KyungHyang*, and *Yeosung Dong-Ah*) were selected for the analysis. These three monthlies are among the top six women's magazines in Korea. *Yeosung Dong-Ah* accounts for 7% (the largest) of the total women's magazine sales in Korea, *Women Sense* accounts for 6.6% (the third largest), and *Lady KyungHyang* accounts for 4.1% (sixth largest). All three magazines cover various topics such as fashion, skin care, home furnishing, and daily-life information. *Lady KyungHyang* was selected for this study because its readers are much younger—mostly in their 20s—in contrast to the readers of the two other magazines, which target readers of 30 years of age and older, according to the Korea Audit Bureau of Circulation in 2003.

We analyzed one issue of each magazine to identify the dominant images of women used in the ads. When there was more than one model present, we used the dominant or larger model for our analysis.

The coding system we developed for this study included several basic and fundamental variables such as product category, race of model, beauty type of model, gaze of model, and occupational role of model (the role that each model represents in the context of the ad).

For example, we were able to identify five beauty types portrayed by the models: classic/elegant, sensual/sexy, cute, trendy, and others. The following briefly describes the characteristics of each beauty type.

1. Classic/elegant: The model has a look considered "classic" in Korean culture. She is slightly older than the average fashion model, usually wearing soft-colored, feminine apparel without being heavily accessorized.
3. Sensual/sexy: The model is sexually attractive. She is wearing sexy attire and may be shot in a variety of suggestive poses (where the chest is thrust forward and the back is arched, for example).
3. Cute: The model is casually attired and youthful in appearance— the "girl next door" look—healthy and active.
4. Trendy: The model wears faddish clothes and displays oversized accessories, is colorfully attired and often with wild or tousled hair.
5. Other: This includes beauty types that did not fall into any of the above categories.

For the occupational role of the models, we used five specific categories:

1. Professional: Women business executives and women with careers or identified jobs.
2. Entertainer/celebrity: Television personnel, movie actresses, and comedians.
3. Family type/homemaker.
4. Recreational: Sporty types, showing some athletic aspects.
5. Decorative: Just looking pretty, with no identified role.

For the race of the models, we used broad categories, based mostly on the physical attributes (e.g., skin color and hair) of each model:

1. Korean.
2. Caucasian: Mostly white models.
3. African: Black models.

No specific distinctions were made for potential Hispanic models.

The sample of three magazines yielded a total of 258 advertisements that contained female models. Ninety-five ads (36.8% of the total sample) were featured in *Woman Sense*, 68 ads (26.4%) in *Lady KyungHyung*, 95 ads (36.8%) in *Yeosung Dong-Ah*.

RESULTS

Overall, the classic/elegant image (56%) was the dominant beauty type depicted in Korean magazine ads, followed by sex kitten/sensual images (31%). About half of all women's images in Korean magazines used a classic/elegant portrayal (dignified and sophisticated, but not heavily accessorized). This can be interpreted as reflecting the traditional, conservative values that Korean society most respects in women.

We found some interesting facts when we examined this portrayal by the race of the models used. The majority of classic/elegant images were represented by Korean models (83%), and 63% of the Korean models in all the ads were used for this image type. In sharp contrast, Caucasian models were heavily used for sex kitten/sensual images (59% of all Caucasians), followed by classic/elegant images (38%), whereas only 21% of the Korean models were posed for sex kitten/sensual images. There was only one ad that used African models that showed sex kitten/sensual images. Since the Korean government started allowing foreign models to appear in advertisements in the early 1990s, models from other races have increasingly been used to attract the reader's attention to advertisements. Caucasian and African models are frequently used to represent seductive and sexy images—mostly to promote lingerie or diet-related products. In addition, 71% of all Korean models' gaze was straight at the camera, whereas 56% of all Caucasian models were posed looking away from the camera, which in this context implies a more seductive look. The strong association of Korean models gazing directly towards the camera invokes another traditional, idealized image of Korean women: submissive, obedient, passive, and calm—not rebellious.

When we examined the association of race with product categories, we found that Korean models were used more commonly to promote certain types of products than were models of other races. Particularly, all the food or food products ads used Korean models exclusively. This reflects the tendency of Koreans to prefer food products originally grown or manufactured in Korea, and their preference for home-cooked meals. By contrast, the women's clothing and women's accessories categories used the highest number of foreign models (68% of all ads in this category) compared with Korean models (32%) (see Appendix, Table 3.1).

In every product category (with the sole exception of women's clothing and accessories), classic/elegant images were used most frequently, followed by sex kitten/sensual images. For example, 59% of all beauty/personal care product ads used classic/elegant images, whereas only 35% of them used sex kitten/sensual images. However, 80% of women's clothing ads (20 ads out of the 25) used sensual images to appeal to their target audience, and one of the women's accessories ads also used this image.

The most popular occupational role portrayed in Korean magazines was the decorative/pretty image (about 51% of all occupational roles), followed by entertainer/celebrity (29.8%), family type/homemaker (5.4%), professional (5.0%), and recreational/sporty (3.9%). Decorative and passive roles for women, with no specific jobs depicted, dominate the magazine ads. These findings support those of recent research such as Chung's (1997, 2001) and Han's (2002) studies, which found that professional and recreational/ sporty roles are only presented in a limited number of ads.

When we compared the occupational role portrayed by the models with the portrayed images of women in the ads, other interesting aspects were revealed. Forty-four percent of classic/elegant images portrayed the decorative/pretty role, and 73% of sex kitten/sensual images presented the decorative/pretty role. This result is consistent with previous findings that women were being portrayed as sex objects or as decorations for men.

When occupational roles represented in magazine ads were compared by product category (see Table 3.2), most product categories predominantly used decorative/pretty roles as the primary image. Entertainer/celebrity was the second most used role. Fifty-seven percent of all beauty and personal care products adopted the decorative/pretty role, and 69% of all medicine/other drugs ads used this role. This finding is of particular interest because "medicine/other drugs" as a product category is considered to be a "hard" or "rational" product, and the advertising world has a tendency to match "hard" products (e.g., computers, technology-oriented products, and medicine) with rational appeals. In this case, products in the medicine category ads were matched with "soft" appeals using decorative/pretty roles. In contrast, food/food products ads promoted their products through entertainer/celebrities (62%), followed by family type/homemaker (24%) and decorative role (14%). All three cleaning products ads used either the entertainer/celebrity or the family type/homemaker role.

DISCUSSION AND CONCLUSION

The results of our study show that the portrayal of women in Korean women's magazines is in accordance with the traditional gender stereotypes identified by previous studies in the United States as well as in Korea and other Asian countries. The predominant image of beauty depicted in Korean magazine ads was classic/elegant. This was followed by sex kitten/sensual images. By using Korean models, the classic/elegant image reflects the ideal beauty that the Korean culture aspires to for its women. Traditional values and feminine traits—calm, charming, soft, caring, and devoted—remain the most desirable. This classic or elegant beauty image was strongly associated with cleaning products, beauty and personal care products, and food and food products, and portrayed "decorative or pretty roles." The ads shown in Figures 3.1 and 3.2 represent the typical classic or elegant beauty type.

The ad for ENPRANI cosmetics uses a Korean model with light make-up, gazing straight at the camera, and with little body exposure. This model is surrounded by light pink roses to highlight a clean, beautiful, and elegant image. The headline says, "The 20s, Forever! ENTRANI." The ad in Figure 3.2 presents a similar image. The ad is for Taster's Choice coffee, and a well-known Korean actress takes a comfortable pose with a smiling, soft, and elegant gaze.

*Figure 3.1. ENPRANI cosmetics ad
(from Yeosung Dong-Ah)*

*Figure 3.2. Taster's Choice ad
(from Yeosung Dong-Ah)*

Another ad appearing in *Yeosung Dong-Ah* (Figure 3.3) presents the typical traditional Confucian ideal for mothers. This ad is for a special medicine, Long Key Bone, which is designed to facilitate children's growth. The headline and body copy in the right upper corner highlight the mother's duties expected within Korean cultural values. It says, "A Mother's Pledge: I pledge to do my best with all my body and heart to improve my children's health and to build a bright future for them."

These associations deliver the message that classic and elegant women should be confined to the domestic sphere and become respectful daughters, good mothers, and sacrificing wives. In other words, these images reinforce the traditional ideology of family values and gender relationships. "Good" Korean women should be calm, quiet, and submissive, physically beautiful and attractive, and should not provoke any problems or conflicts.

Out of six categories of occupational role, the decorative/pretty role was the most popular depiction in the magazine ads in our sample. Forty-four percent of the classic/elegant images showed a decorative/pretty role,

Figure 3.3. "*Long Key Bone*" *ad* (from *Yeosung Dong-Ah*)

73% of sex kitten/sensual images were presented in the decorative/pretty role. This result is consistent with most of the previous findings that women were represented as passive or as decorations for men. As recent research by Han (2002) and Chung (1997) reveals, and this study confirms, active roles for women (e.g., professional and recreational) are now being seen in magazine advertisements. There is no doubt, however, that those images are still very limited in number and continue to be overshadowed by the predominance of decorative and passive role depictions.

Another interesting finding of our study is how foreign models are being used in Korean women's magazine ads. Foreign models (mostly Caucasian) are far more frequently posed with a seductive and indirect gaze to present images of sensual sex kittens than are Korean models. Foreign models feature most often in ads for women's clothing (mostly underwear or lingerie products), beauty and personal care products, and women's accessories, whereas they never appear in ads for food products. The ad in Figure 3.4 is for Wacoal bra and appeared in *Woman Sense* magazine. Unlike in the ads in Figures 3.1 and 3.2, the Western model's body is more exposed, and she has an indirect, seductive gaze. The ad in Figure 3.5 is for Triumph bra, and the three Western models in this ad seem to be enjoying their lives and they look active and happy. These two ads also portray active and confident images, images that ads with Korean models do not present.

Figure 3.4. Wacoal ad (from Woman Sense)

Figure 3.5. Triumph ad (from Woman Sense)

This representation by foreign models reflects the direction of current changes in the attitudes of young Korean women. They now consider Western beauty superior to traditional Korean beauty and associate Western fashion and style with advanced and modern beauty ideals. Such representation reinforces the dominant patriarchal ideology and traditional values by showing Korean women to be conservative, passive, and domesticated, while at the same time portraying foreign models as wild, sensual, sexy, aggressive, seductive, and liberal. It will be interesting to observe how rapidly the globalization of the Korean media and culture through advertising and other cultural products accelerates these stereotypes of Western women and Western beauty among young Koreans.

Our findings are not surprising in spite of the fact that magazine advertisements are supposedly not meant to serve as social primers or agents of social changes. At face value, they are designed to naturalize people and things in such a way as to maximize demand, but in doing so, they define social relations in terms of the consumption of goods and services.

Women seeing such advertisements are more likely to accept the patriarchal ideology inherent in the text: that is, it is the women's job to look appealing and to accept what is given to them without dispute. The overall message from the representation of women in this type of Korean advertising is that women must make an effort to conform to the traditional notion of femininity. It projects women as mere bodies rather than as full persons, available as objects existing for the pleasure and profit of men (Roy, 1998).

Besides what is represented in the ads, the equally important issue is what has not been represented in the media. As we noted earlier, Korean women—particularly younger women and lower-class women—have contributed enormously to the Korean economic "miracle" by playing a major role in the workforce that has fueled industrialization and economic development. Despite their contribution, these women are still not seen in the same light as "traditional" Korean women. Media images of females at work are greatly outnumbered by the images of women in traditional, domesticated roles used in advertising. Thus, the majority of media images of Korean women remain confined to traditional household settings or as decorations with no apparent working roles. This portrayal also reinforces the unmistakable division of labor in Korean society.

Our analysis of the women's images represented in Korean magazines leads us to conclude that this constructed reality is far different from the actual dynamic and transforming reality of women in Korean society. The debate over the role of advertising as a "simple social reflector" or as "social/cultural creator" even becomes irrelevant because advertising is apparently so slow to reflect the dynamics of changing Korean society. Our current study suggests that advertising maintains the dominant ideology of Korean society by failing to represent accurately the ongoing conflicts and challenges facing Korean women. Hence, Korean advertising presents a limited version of reality. Although sometimes including superficial representation of active and professional women, advertising leaves the underlying ideological foundation untouched and unchallenged. At the same time, advertising perpetuates stereotypical images of Western beauty by strongly associating foreign models with sensual images and seductive gazes.

To change the stereotypical portrayal of women in Korean advertising, public education is needed. This would enable women to exercise their power as consumers by boycotting inappropriately advertised products. Women in Korea must become aware of their power as the country's largest group of purchasers of goods and services.

Based on our exploratory study into the portrayal of women in Korean magazine ads, we offer three suggestions for further study. First, future studies could compare female images with the male images in advertising: our study only focused on female images. Second, different types of magazines (e.g., fashion, home design, and business magazines) and series of publication years could be considered for comparative studies of differences and trends in gender portrayal. Finally, instead of relying on content analysis alone, we suggest that in-depth textual analysis using semiotics could be added to uncover the deeper meanings embedded in advertising.

APPENDIX

Table 3.1.
Race by Product Category (%, *N*)

	BEAUTY/ PERSONAL CARE	MEDICINE/ DRUGS	WOMEN'S CLOTHING	FOOD/ FOOD PRODUCTS	CLEANING PRODUCTS	WOMEN'S ACCESSORIES	MISCELLANEOUS
KOREAN	75 (98)	85 (22)	32 (8)	100 (21)	67 (2)	0	77 (40)
CAUCASIAN	25 (32)	15 (4)	64 (16)	0	33 (1)	100 (1)	23 (12)
AFRICAN	0	0	4 (1)	0	0	0	0
TOTAL (*N*)	130	26	25	21	3	1	52

Table 3.2.
Occupational Role of Models by Product Category (%, *N*)

RANK	PRODUCT CATEGORY	DECORATIVE/ LOOKING PRETTY	ENTERTAINER/ CELEBRITY	FAMILY TYPE/ HOMEMAKER	PROFESSIONAL	RECREATION	OTHERS	TOTAL
1	Beauty/Personal Care	57 (74)	28 (37)	0.8 (1)	4 (6)	1.5 (2)	7.7 (10)	130
2	Medicine/Other drugs	69 (18)	12 (3)	7.7 (2)	0	11.5 (3)	0	26
3	Women's Clothing	60 (15)	32 (8)	0	0	8.0 (2)	0	15
4	Food/ Food Products	14 (3)	62 (13)	24 (5)	0	0	0	21
5	Cleaning Products	0	33 (1)	67 (2)		0	0	3
6	Women's Accessories	100 (1)	0	0	0	0	0	1
7	Miscellaneous	40.4 (21)	28.8 (15)	7.7 (4)	13.5 (7)	5.8 (3)	3.8 (2)	52
Total								258

REFERENCES

Asia & Pacific: Strategies to change media portrayal of women. (1990). *Women's International Network News, 16*(1), 45.

Busby, L. J. (1975). Sex role research on the mass media. *Journal of Communication, 25,* 107–131.

Choy, L. I. (2000). Breaking through: A right of passage for feminist artists in Korea. Retrieved October 29, 2000, from www.artwomen.org/jongmyo/article.

Chung, K. H. (1997). Images of women and men in television commercials. *Hankook Bang song Hakbo, 9,* 215–250.

Chung, K. H. (2001). A study on advertising's sexual representation: Focused on print advertisements. *Kwangko Yungoo, 50,* 115–135.

Daehong Communications. (1999). *Koreans: Changes in consumer buying behaviors and lifestyles, 1989–1999. Vol. 1: Teens and Twenties.*

Ewen, S., & Ewen, E. (1992). *Channels of desire: Mass images and the shaping of American consciousness.* Minneapolis: University of Minnesota Press.

Ferguson, J. H., Kreshal, P. J., & Tinkham, S. (1990). In the pages of *Ms.*: Sex role portrayals of women in advertising. *Journal of Advertising, 19*(1), 40–51.

Ford, J. B., Vooli, P. K., Honeycutt Jr., E. D., & Casey, S. L. (1998). Gender role portrayals in Japanese advertising: A magazine content analysis. *Journal of Advertising, 27*(1), 113–125.

Fung, A. (2000). Feminist philosophy and cultural representation in the Asian context. *Gazette, 62*(2), 153–165.

Furnham, A., & Skae, E. (1997). Changes in the stereotypical portrayal of men and women in British television advertisements. *European Psychologist, 2,* 44–51.

Furnham, A., Abramsky, S., & Gunter, B. (1997). A cross-cultural content analysis of children's advertising advertisements. *Sex Roles: A Journal of Research, 37*(1–2), 91–100.

Furnham, A., Mak, T., & Tanidjojo, L. (2000). An Asian perspective on the portrayal of men and women in television advertisements: Studies from Hong Kong and Indonesian television. *Journal of Applied Social Psychology, 30*(11), 2341–2364.

Gilly, M. C. (1988). Sex roles in advertising: A comparison of television advertisements in Australia, Mexico, and the United States. *Journal of Marketing, 52,* 75–85.

Goffman, E. (1979). Gender advertisements. *Critical Studies in Mass Communication, 8,* 333–352.

Goldman, R. (1992). *Reading ads socially.* London: Routledge.

Han, E. K. (2002). A study on the change of masculine and feminine image in advertisements, 1993–1999. *Hankook Bang song Hakbo, 14*(2), 243–277.

Kilbourne, J. (2000). Killing us softly 3: Advertising's image of women [video]. Northampton, MA: Media Education Foundation.

Kim, H. C. (1994). A study on female images represented in magazine advertising. Unpublished master's thesis, Chung-Ang University, Seoul, Korea.

Kim, Y.C. (1979). *Women of Korea: A history from ancient times to 1945.* Seoul: Ewha Womans University Press.

Kolbe, R. H., & Albanese, P. J. (1996). Man to man: A content analysis of sole-male images in male-audience magazines. *Journal of Advertising, 25,* 1–40.

Korea Audit Bureau of Circulation. Retrieved in 2003, from http://www.kabc.or.kr

Korean Advertising Review Board (2004a). Promoting truth in advertising for you. Retrieved September 30, 2004 from http://www.karb.or.kr/e/index.html.

Korean Advertising Review Board (2004b). Self-regulation guidelines. Retrieved September 30, 2004 from http://www.karb.or.kr/data/data03_02.asp

Krassas, N., Blauwkamp, J., & Wesselink, P. (2001). Boxing Helena and corseting Eunice: Sexual rhetoric in *Cosmopolitan* and *Playboy* magazines. *Sex Roles, 44,* 751–771.

McGough, J. C. (2002). Code of advertising standards for Ireland (5th ed.). Retrieved September 25, 2004, from http://www.asai.ie/codes_2002/full.html.

Palley, M. L. (1990). Women's status in South Korea: Tradition and change. *Asian Survey, 30*(12), 1136–1153.

Park, K. A. (1993). Women and development: The case of South Korea. *Comparative Politics, 25,* 127–45.

Reichert, T., Lambiase, J., Margan, S., Carstarphen, M., & Zavoina, S. (1999). Cheesecake and beefcake: No matter how you slice it, sexual explicitness in advertising continues to increase. *Journalism & Mass Communication Quarterly, 76*(1), 7–20.

Roy, A. (1998). Images of domesticity and motherhood in Indian television commercials: A critical study. *Journal of Popular Culture, 32*(3), 117–34.

Rudman, J., & Verdi, P. (1993). Exploitation: Comparing sexual and violent imagery of females and males in advertising. *Women & Health, 20,* 1–14.

Schuman, M. (2001, Feb. 21). Some Korean women go to great lengths to show a little leg—tired of their thick calves, they find surgical solution; kill nerves or cut muscle. *Wall Street Journal,* p. A1.

Soh, C. S. (1993). Sexual equality, male superiority, and Korean women in politics: Changing gender relations in a patriarchal democracy. *Sex Roles, 28*(1/2), 73–90.

Song, J. H. (1991). Comparative analysis of female images in magazine advertising. *Kwangko Yungoo, 40,* 119–145.

4

WOMEN AS TARGET

Internationalization of the Women's Magazine Industry in Taiwan

Ping Shaw

This study examines the internationalization process of the Taiwan women's magazine industry and its effect on the industry itself. The first section explores the growing concentration of ownership and control over the women's magazine industry at the international level by reviewing the major literature. The second section looks at the internationalization process of Taiwan's women's magazine industry. The third section investigates the readership and the influence of internationalization and advertising on Taiwan's women's magazine industry. The final section concerns the commercialization of Taiwan's women's magazines.

Since the late 20th century, one thing is strikingly clear—national economies are becoming increasingly globally integrated. Nowhere is this integration more evident than in the media industries around the world. The 1980s saw the world's economy become more fully deregulated. This trend and a push toward "free market" economies have led to an international consolidation of media companies, and a handful of mammoth private organizations have begun to dominate the world's mass media (Gershon, 1993). As Bagdikian (1989) noted, most of the giant media companies confidently claimed that by the 1990s they—five to ten corporate giants—might control most of the world's important newspapers, magazines, books, broadcast stations, movies, recordings, and videocassettes.

As Bagdikian (1992) further argued, a new global system is integrating worldwide mass media with worldwide mass advertising. What is more, advertising agencies have consolidated into a handful of conglomerates that are following the major world manufacturers of standardized foods, soft drinks, cigarettes, and medicines into new markets. The multinational manufacturers of consumer goods are the ultimate sources of revenue for both global media firms and global advertising agencies. Consumer goods advertising is the major source of profit for most of the new global media firms.

A new player, banking, has joined this global system. The dominant mass media firms have become so large that their financing, credit, interlocked directors, and sometimes their ownership intertwine them with the world's largest banks and investment houses. The resulting troika—global media corporations, multinational manufacturers, and worldwide banking—represents a new power in world politics (Bagdikian, 1992).

The giant media firms aim to capture market share: Once one or two of these media giants occupy a substantial part of any market, as Bagdikian (1992, p. 243) argued, they have strong power "in setting prices and altering the product without fear of significant competition." In the case of the media, Bagdikian noted that "market" is the world, and "product" is the news, information, and popular culture.

The giants also aim for maximum synergism, that is, they aim for control of as many different media as possible: news, magazines, radio, television, books, motion pictures, cable systems, satellite channels, and so on (Bagdikian, 1992). Time Warner, for example, is the largest media corporation in the United States, with media revenue estimated by *Advertising Age* ("100 Leading Media Companies," 1998) to be $13.27 billion in 1997. It has significant ownership interests in magazines, radio, television, books, motion pictures, cable, recordings, and the production and syndication of programming for other media firms as well as for its own outlets. Time Warner is one of the largest U.S. cable companies and one of the largest book publishers in the world. It is also the largest magazine publisher in the United States, owning *Time*, *Life*, *Fortune*, *People*, and *Sports Illustrated*, among other titles (Bagdikian, 2000; Ledbetter, 1996). As Bagdikian (1992) estimated, its aggregate worldwide readership exceeds 120 million.

The large publishing groups have consolidated their control over the magazine markets. This market domination appears to confer a number of advantages that, as Driver and Gillespie noted, include:

> the revenue benefits associated with maximizing audiences across titles, the cost advantages associated with bulk print buying, the power conferred by control over distribution channels, the command over resources necessary to launch, market and sustain new titles, or to acquire them, the spreading of risks through diversification and cross-

media ownership, and the ability to reap the rewards of spreading successful publishing formulas across national markets. (1993, p. 199)

As a result, media giants make more profit from each invested dollar
than smaller firms. For example, in its 1987 annual report, Time Inc. said,
"[o]ur competitors . . . can't duplicate the reach and clout of the eight magazines we're offering our advertisers" (cited in Bagdikian, 1989, p. 185).

If the Time Inc. annual report statement carries any truth, the question
then becomes, what choices remain for the competitors—especially the local
companies that serve readers of unique demographic and cultural characteristics? The purpose of this study is to examine the internationalization
process of Taiwan's women's magazine industry and to describe the effect it
is having on the industry.

THE INTERNATIONAL EXPANSION
OF WOMEN'S MAGAZINES

Many women's magazines are subsidiaries of large media conglomerates. By
the 1980s, the women's magazine industry had become thoroughly integrated into the international communication system. This development inter-
twines the concentration of ownership at the domestic level and international expansion with the growing importance of advertising as a major financial
source.

The tightening concentration has been the most dramatic in the U.S.
magazine industry sector; between 1981 to 1988, according to Bagdikian's
(2000) calculations, the 20 dominant corporations became only three. These
three magazine giants, in order of estimated annual revenues, are Time
Warner, News Corporation, and Hearst. Among the three, Hearst is the primary publisher of women's magazines. It publishes several women's magazines: *Cosmopolitan, Good Housekeeping, Harper's Bazaar, House
Beautiful, Redbook, Town and Country, Victoria,* and *Marie Claire* (the latter jointly owned by Hearst and the French firm, Marie Claire Album SA),
most of which have wide circulations and huge revenues. In addition to
magazines, Hearst owns a broad range of other media interests in the United
States and abroad, including television, radio, movies, video, newspapers,
and books (McCracken, 1993).

Through mergers and takeovers, the magazine industry has become
increasingly transnational in scope, as particular companies become integrated into large communication conglomerates that span the globe. Since as
early as the 1960s, North American publishers have seen the advantage of
using the capital and publishing expertise acquired in one country as a basis

for entry into the market elsewhere. To attract advertisers, they promoted women's magazines as an effective means of reaching women in Third World countries to sell goods in expanding markets (McCracken, 1983).

U.S. publishers have been active in other parts of the world. Hearst has long been involved in overseas publishing, either by direct ownership or through the licensing of its titles to local publishers. *Good Housekeeping* was launched in the United States in 1885, arrived in Britain in 1922, and was followed there by *Harper's Bazaar* in 1929. *Good Housekeeping* has Japanese, Australian, and South American editions. *Cosmopolitan* was an example of licensing efficiency when Hearst recognized that the Helen Gurley Brown formula born in 1964 was eminently exportable. When the British version proved so successful, Hearst swiftly followed up by selling licenses to publishers in South America, Japan, the Netherlands, France, Italy, Germany, Australia, South Africa, Greece, and Hong Kong (Barrell & Braithwaite, 1988; Zomosa, 1983). Condé Nast is also active in international publishing, both with foreign subsidiaries and through licensing. *Vogue's* British, Italian, and French editions are directly owned, and the Australian edition is published under license (Compaine, 1982).

European groups, especially French and German, have also internationalized themselves extensively. France's Hachette claimed that nearly 50% of its total income in 1988 came from outside France (*"Hachette Says Half . . . ,"* 1989). Its weekly, *Elle,* granted a license for a Japanese edition in 1969, and five years later for an Arabic language edition. By 1990, versions of *Elle* had also appeared in Brazil, West Germany, China, Greece, and Hong Kong. Another French weekly, *Marie Claire,* went abroad in the late 1970s and within five years brought out five international editions (Mattelart, 1991).

The owner of the German magazine *Burda* launched a British edition in 1973. The Bertelsmann group introduced *Geo* in Germany in 1976 and set a new pattern by competing with the U.S. and Canadian publishers on their own terrain when they launched both French and North American editions in 1979 (Mattelart, 1991).

The internationalization of women's magazines has been largely through franchising. Because a women's magazine is unlikely to be adaptable to every country, many have foreign editions that can differ considerably from the parent publication. The franchising strategy often came about as a resolution to the conflict between domestic cultural needs and international media output. Through the franchise system, the title's proprietor cedes the right to use the name of a title to a national publisher—under specific conditions and in exchange for the payment of royalties. The franchise allows a local publisher—the concessionary—to launch the new title without excessive outlay and with low risk of failure. The concessionary benefits from a brand name, a reputation, a format, and the know-how—the fruit of many years of experience. The concessionary thus connects with a transnational network and from the start acquires contacts with advertisers already accustomed to purchasing space in the parent magazine and thus predisposed to advertising in the local offshoot. Sometimes the local publisher is given the opportunity to participate in regular brainstorming sessions with editors of other local editions (Mattelart, 1991).

The target envisaged by local versions of international publications is mainly the upper reaches of the middle class, defined here by purchasing power. The formula of *Buenhogar*, the Latin American edition of *Good Housekeeping*, according to its editor, was "directed at young, modern married Latin Americans with good education and housing. Their interests are no different from their North American equivalents." Similarly, the target of *Marie Claire* international editions was the stereotypical "young western urban woman: active woman of 18–30, who travels abroad" (Mattelart, 1991, pp. 72–73).

As I mentioned above, advertising plays a significant role in the world's media systems. On a global scale, the mass media serve advertisers as a channel of access to large numbers of consumers. In fact, industrial globalization would not have been possible without a global system of mass media and marketing tools capable of efficiently handling global operations. As Janus (1981) noted, the 1960s and 1970s witnessed growth in consumer magazines in several regions of the world, especially in Europe, the Middle East, and parts of Latin America and Africa. These magazines grew in direct proportion to the advertising support available to them.

As Santa Cruz and Erazo (1980, cited in McCracken, 1983) argued, transnational advertising continues to provide the primary financial backing of women's magazines in Latin America. In the 27 magazines of six Latin American countries they studied, 59% of the ads were for transnational goods and services. Of the 18 most-advertised product categories, 13 included a majority of transnational brands. The highest incidence of transnational advertising occurred in the beauty products (90%) and fashion (56%) categories. And beauty products ads were the most frequent category found in the expensive space on the back and inside covers. Indeed, Santa Cruz and Erazo aptly termed contemporary women's magazines, "women's advertising magazines."

The dependence of the women's magazine industry on advertising subsidies, according to Earnshaw (1984), has two main effects on magazine content. The first is the pressure on editors to produce publications with appeal to the audiences that advertisers want to reach. The second effect is the pressure on journalists to provide a suitable, persuasive environment within the magazine for the sale of advertisers' products.

Advertising has played a crucial role in shaping the form and content of women's magazines since the 1880s, according to Damon-Moore and

Kaestle (1991). The strong relationship between advertising and women's magazines has been clear from the beginning: Women were viewed as the primary consumers of products, magazines were conceived as platforms for national advertisements aimed at women, and traditional women-targeted advertising and magazines alike have flourished ever since. This pattern has held for over a hundred years and shows no signs of shifting in the near future. This relationship is durable and circular: For women, magazines provide a gender-targeted forum, and, in turn, advertising supports those magazines that best showcase their messages.

As this brief survey demonstrates, magazine publishing has become much more a part of the integrated and international media economy. Western magazine publishers, searching for new audiences and new sources of revenue, acquired interests in other countries, especially in Third World countries. Next, I explore the impact of the internationalization process on the women's magazine industry in Taiwan.

INTERNATIONALIZATION OF THE WOMEN'S MAGAZINE INDUSTRY IN TAIWAN

Taiwan has vigorously entered the international capitalist system, despite being politically isolated from the international community. Its strong economic growth has created a growing, affluent middle class that has attracted the attention of multinational consumer-product giants, among them Unilever (an Anglo-Dutch firm), Procter & Gamble (the U.S. consumer products giant), and Nestlé (the Swiss food and beverages conglomerate). These manufacturers in turn encouraged their advertising agencies to enter Taiwan to service their accounts, often with a global strategy. Since 1985, the influx of multinational advertising agencies has transformed Taiwan's advertising industry. More than 20 transnational advertising agencies, including J. Walter Thompson, Ogilvy & Mather, and McCann-Erickson from the United States, Dentsu from Japan, and the U.K.-based Saatchi & Saatchi, established affiliations with local agencies or set up branch offices in Taiwan (Goldstein, 1989; Hu, 1998).

The interrelated growth of international industry, advertising, and magazines has become quite evident in Taiwan. In the case of glossy Chinese-language editions of international women's magazines, the cultural text is addressed primarily to Taiwanese women because they are responsible for a good deal of consumer goods and services purchasing. International women's magazines perform important functions for transnational corporations—both for those owning the magazines and those advertising in them. Publishers have promoted these women's magazines as an especially effective means of reaching Taiwanese women to sell goods in an expanding market. For example, in an advertisement from *Brain* in 1993, *Elle* tells advertisers that its readers are "the consumers who have the highest consuming power." Similarly, in another *Brain* ad the same year, *Marie Claire* claims that it can attract female readers "that are independent and have a high consumption ability."

The major international women's magazines in Taiwan are listed in Table 4.1 (see Appendix). International women's periodicals have varied financial investment structures: joint ventures, licensing agreements, or foreign branches. *Cosmopolitan*, for example, was first introduced in Taiwan in 1989: A Hong Kong publisher who owned the license to publish the Chinese edition of *Cosmopolitan* organized the first magazine joint venture in Taiwan. However, this joint venture failed year later, and Hua Shang Cultural Enterprise, Inc. acquired the license to *Cosmopolitan* in 1992 and began a joint venture in 1995 with Hearst, the parent company. Soon to follow were several other transnational magazines from Western countries, including *Harper's Bazaar* (U.S.), *Elle* (France), and *Marie Claire* (France).

The Chinese-language editions of international women's magazines published in Taiwan have benefited from the significant financial support of transnational advertisers in Taiwan. Domestic magazines, by contrast, do not have the same advantages. An example of this kind of structured support, Interderco, a subsidiary of Hachette, is responsible for supporting the global editions of *Elle* magazine and helps them gain the support of large advertisers ("*Elle* is founded in October," 1991). Moreover, the international brand names alone are often enough to attract the attention of transnational companies. When *Marie Claire* first published in Taiwan in 1993, for instance, some transnational cosmetic companies such as Elizabeth Arden, Estée Lauder, and Guerlain claimed to have set aside some of their advertising budgets in preparation to support it ("The Beautiful Start of *Marie Claire*," 1993).

Table 4.2 (Appendix) ranks the largest Taiwan women's magazines by advertising revenue. Among them, the transnational women's magazines — *Vogue*, *Elle*, and *Marie Claire* — share the bulk of Taiwan women's magazine advertising revenues; they entered the market only fifteen or so years ago. *Nong-nong*, which now relies mostly on advertising for its financial support, is the leader among the domestic women's magazines able to compete with transnational magazines for advertising revenues. In 1996, the publisher of *Nong-nong* reported that 77% of its revenues came from advertising and 23% from subscription and retail sales (*Nong-nong*, 1994).

Many of the traditional domestic magazines are falling behind in the competition with transnational periodicals for advertising profits and may eventually have to close down. In contrast, though, several newer domestic titles targeted to young women have already prospered since coming onto the market in the late 1990s. *Sugar* and *Beauty* are the most prominent examples.

Taiwan's leading women's magazines are ranked by readership in Table 4.3 (Appendix). The magazines at the top of the rankings appeal mostly to Taiwan's well-educated, urban middle-class women with good jobs. In turn, their power as consumers with high salaries appeals to advertisers. Not surprisingly, women's magazines are almost exclusively targeted to female readers, and at least 78% of readers are female. Most readers are young women aged 21–30 (from 34% to 64%), with undergraduate level education (at least 50%). They often have jobs in commerce, finance, or the service sector (from 42% to 66%); only a small portion of them are housewives (fewer than 18%). Thus they command good salaries, most of them earning NT $20,000–50,000 (US $600–1,515) per month. Finally, most of these readers live in the more urbanized, northern part of Taiwan.

The characteristics of the readership of the domestic magazines (*Beauty* and *Nong-nong*) and that of the international women's magazines (*Cosmopolitan*, *Marie Claire*, and *Elle*) are quite different. The international magazines have an older and wealthier readership than domestic magazines. For example, more than a third of the readers of international titles are over 30, whereas only 26% or fewer of *Nong-nong* and *Beauty* readers are 30 or older. Added to that, more readers of *Marie Clair* and *Cosmopolitan* earn over NT$50,000 per month (35% and 21%, respectively) than *Nong-nong* and *Beauty* (15% and none, respectively).

CONTENT ANALYSIS OF ADVERTISEMENTS IN TAIWAN WOMEN'S MAGAZINES

As I related earlier, advertising has become a major financial source for women's publications in Taiwan—especially in the wake of the internationalization of the industry. We should therefore examine the contents of the advertisements in Taiwan's women's magazines to further our understanding of the influence of internationalization and advertising on the women's magazine industry in the country.

Methodology

I selected two domestic women's magazines and two Chinese-language editions of international titles for content analysis. The domestic periodicals were *Beauty* and *Nong-nong*, and the international magazines were *Cosmopolitan* and *Elle*. These monthly magazines all have large nationwide readerships. Two 2003 issues of each magazine—eight issues in all—were analyzed for this study. Only full-page or larger advertisements qualified for analysis. Smaller advertisements were excluded because of the focus of the study on products that major advertisers felt worthy of heavy advertising expenditures. In all, 608 advertisements were analyzed.

The classification system was based on a coding scheme I used in an earlier study (Shaw, 1999). The scheme includes the number of pages occupied, product categories, and product origins. The product categories were beauty and personal products, clothing and accessories, foods and beverages, fitness, home appliances and electronics, books and magazines, as well as others (medicine, travel, cars, credit cards, entertainment, photo studio, cigarettes, and so on). The product origins were grouped as domestic, transnational, and joint venture.

Results

Table 4.4 (Appendix) lists the major findings of the content analysis. *Elle* and *Nong-nong* devoted more space to full-page advertisements (25%, 44%, 40%, and 30%, respectively) than *Beauty* and *Cosmopolitan* (30% and 25%, respectively). In addition, these four magazines frequently ran single advertisements spanning more than one page.

As for product category, beauty and personal products were the most common in all four magazines. Surprisingly, as Table 4.4 indicates, domestic titles devoted more space to beauty products than the international ones. Whereas more than 60% of advertisements in domestic magazines were for cosmetics, perfume, and sanitary products (84% in *Beauty*, and 67% *in Nong-nong*), over 40% of the ads in international titles were for beauty products (55% in *Cosmopolitan*, and 40% *in Elle*). Clothing and accessories was the second most common advertisement category in *Elle* (46%), *Cosmopolitan* (29%), and *Nong-nong* (11%).

Strikingly, over three-quarters of all advertisements in all four titles were for the products of transnational corporations. About 90% of the ads in *Elle* and *Beauty* (90% and 88%, respectively) were for transnational products, whereas about 80% of the ads in *Nong-nong* and *Cosmopolitan* were for transnational brands. These products were primarily for cosmetics, perfume, and clothing and accessories from high-priced luxury brands such as Guerlain, Lancôme, Elizabeth Arden, Christian Dior, Chanel, Cartier, and Tiffany.

Table 4.5 (Appendix) shows the breakdown of product category by product origin. As shown, all product categories include a majority of transnational brands. The greatest amount of transnational advertising is for clothing and accessories, food and beverages, and others (100%), and advertisements in the beauty and personal products category were also primarily for transnational brands (74.7%).

Moreover, I found in this analysis of Taiwanese women's magazine advertisements that the predominant stereotype is of women in aesthetic roles. Portrayals of women as aesthetic objects form one of the most profitable stereotypes used in Taiwan's magazine ads. Advertisers have found again and again that this stereotypical portrayal successfully sells their products.

As shown in the content analysis above, currently, we can see there are no differences between local and international women's periodicals in Taiwan, in terms of the product categories advertised and the product origins. Both domestic and global women's magazines promote a wide range of transnational luxury products to Taiwan's women and earn revenue from global advertising. These products are mainly beauty and fashion goods, and their advertisements transmit Western beauty culture values to Taiwan's society. It can be expected that this would bear some effects on local women's culture. In the age of globalization, women's magazines, whether they are local or global ones, should be seen as the site of negotiation between local and global forces.

THE COMMODIFICATION
OF TAIWAN WOMEN'S MAGAZINES

During the early 1980s, although women's magazines in Taiwan may not have labeled themselves as feminist, nevertheless many attempted to address women's needs for self-awareness, self-realization, and the development of women's culture. Aside from the journals targeted at young factory workers, a few prestigious magazines, including *Women's Magazine*, often focused on issues of women's welfare and their roles in society (Shaw, 2000).

The situation changed in the late 1980s, however, as internationalization and advertising penetration began to cast a large combined effect on the women's magazine industry. The closer linkage between Taiwan women's magazines and advertising was a major development in the 1990s. Advertisements began to form the most important source of revenue for women's magazines. Through the process of internationalization, Taiwan's women's magazines have become increasingly dependent on advertising revenues. Moreover, transnational advertising as a portion of total advertising has also increased. Since internationalization, the importance of women's magazines as global advertising tools has shaped their development. The major changes in the Taiwanese women's magazine industry, associated with the expansion of international women's magazines and advertising, are the commodification of the audience, the magazine content, and of the industry as a whole.

Women's magazines in Taiwan have completed their passage through the process of commercialization: They now serve as tools for advertisers to sell their goods while they sell their readers to advertisers. As political economist Dallas Smythe (1981) argued, the principle product of the media is audiences.

> The secret of the growth of Consciousness Industry in the past century will be found in (1) the relation of advertising to the news, entertainment, and information material in the mass media; (2) the relations of both that material and advertising to real consumer goods and services, political candidates, and public issues; (3) the relations of advertising and consumer goods and services to the people who consume them; (4) the effective control of people's lives which the monopoly capitalist corporations dominating the forging three sets of relationships try to establish and maintain. . . . The commercial mass media are advertising in their entirety . . . both advertising and the "program material" reflect, mystify, and are essential to the sale of goods and services. (Smythe, 1981, p. 8)

Women's magazines in Taiwan—now commercial media, as described by Smythe—mediate between advertisers and audiences and successfully deliver the "right" audience to advertisers. Their target audience is urban middle- and upper-class women, well educated, working outside the home, with above-average salaries, and, most importantly, possessing superior buying power. This is the audience of greatest interest to advertisers, and these magazines deliver luxury product advertisements precisely to these women. According to my content analysis, among all the product categories, beauty and personal products as well as clothing and accessories are the most frequently advertised transnational products. Moreover, these categories of consumer goods are also the most highly advertised in the magazines overall, and in the case of beauty products, they most frequently occupy the expensive space on the back and inside covers.

An examination of the content of commercialized women's magazines in Taiwan shows that the boundary between advertising and editorial matter is becoming indistinct. The largest advertisers, generating the greatest portion of a magazine's revenues, receive the strongest support in the form of product and brand recommendations in editorial space. These recommendations are an especially effective form of advertising because the products or services appear to have been chosen objectively by the editors, whereas in reality, they exploit readers' trust in the editors' knowledge and objectivity.

The editorial structure of women's magazines further supports paid-for advertising by presenting showplaces, values, and themes with strong affinities to the ads. Today in most of Taiwan's women's magazines, advertising and editorial content form a continuum, especially in the category of beauty and fashion. Like the advertising content, the major portion of the editorial content in women's magazines consists of beauty and fashion. In an earlier study we found that between 1998 and 2002 this category took up more than 80% of the advertising space in the young women's magazines, *Beauty* and *Jasmine* (Shaw & Wu, 2004). We also saw that in the fashion and beauty sections—where most of the consumer advertising is to be found—magazines use female images almost exclusively. From their youth, Taiwanese women are taught by their magazines that the secret of success lies in physical appearance. Encouraging women to aspire to and strive towards beauty and fashion ideals is an important function of these magazines—as vehicles for fashion and beauty advertising.

Using Western fantasies of modernity is a strategy frequently employed by publishers of women's magazines in Asia to promote sales (Hayashi, 1995). In another study (Shaw, 1997), I showed that to accommodate this materialistic, consumption-based Western fantasy, the transnational magazines in Taiwan, emphasize individual-centered lifestyles that feature new ways to dress and to apply make-up. The magazines represent beauty to be Western fashion, style, and individuality. Free to indulge in a narcissism based on Western fantasy, readers can for a moment forget their actual appearance in the mirror, replacing that memory with the magazine's concrete examples of ideal Western beauty (Shaw, 1997).

As an advertising medium, transnational periodicals have become more powerful than domestic women's magazines. They have established the model for all other women's publications in Taiwan by using modern printing techniques, high-quality paper, glossy covers, and sophisticated advertising techniques. Now locally owned magazines, too, emphasize that they have international, modern views on fashion. An additional influence on the shape of women's magazines is the changes they undergo in preparation for carrying more luxury product advertising. The domestic magazine with the highest circulation, *New Woman*, for example, had not been able to attract transnational advertisers, according to its editor-in-chief, because its popular compact size was less suitable for presenting products in ads than the large-format magazines. In 1997, for the sake of financial security, its format was changed to the same large size as transnational magazines. In spite of this, however, its worsening financial situation forced its closure three years later.

By aspiring to becoming vehicles for big advertising money, women's magazines have themselves become commodities to be bought and sold in the media marketplace. For instance, Hua-Shie Cultural Enterprise, Inc., the publisher of the Chinese-language edition of *Elle*, sold back its 49% ownership of the magazine to the parent company Hachette for NT $735 million ("The Joint-Ventured *Elle* Magazine Will Be Broken Up," 1995). Furthermore, Hua-Shie sold three of its companies involved in public relations, cultural enterprises, and publishing to Condé Nast Publications, the U.S.-based transnational media company ("CNP Group Merged," 1996).

As commodities, Taiwan's women's magazines will become more and more attractive to transnational media conglomerates in the future, not only because of the booming market in Taiwan, but also because the Chinese-language market is already large and continues to expand. Greater China—that massive community located in mainland China, Taiwan, Hong Kong, Singapore, and Malaysia—shares the same language and cultural identity, and its potential to develop economically is hard to estimate (Frith & Tsao, 1998). This means that routes for rapid entry into this immense market are becoming important to the multinational giants. The domestic women's magazine industry in Taiwan, through its integration with the international capitalist system, will continue to face increasing foreign competition, and future research could focus on the impact of the internationalization of the magazine industry on local women's culture.

Table 4.1.

International Women's Magazines in Taiwan: Ownership and Licensing

MAGAZINE	FOUNDED	AFFILIATE	TAIWAN PUBLISHER	COOPERATION TYPE
Cosmopolitan	1989	Hearst (U.S.)	1. Nong-nong Magazine, Inc. (1989–1990) 2. Hong Kong's Hsing-Shi Company (1991–1992) 3. Hua-Shang Cultural Enterprise, Inc. (since 1992)	1. Joint venture with H.K. licensee 2. Joint venture (since 1995) 3. Licensee (1992–1995), joint venture (since 1995)
Harper's Bazaar	1990	Hearst (U.S.)	1. Hua-Shang Cultural Enterprise, Inc. 2. Hwa-Ker Publishing Co. (since 1995)	1. Licensee 2. Joint venture (since 1995)
Elle	1991	Hachette (France)	1. Hua-Shie Cultural Enterprise, Inc. (1991–1996) 2. Hachette Subsidiary	1. Joint venture (Hachette 51%, Hua-Shie 49%) 2. Hachette 100% (since 1996)
Marie Claire	1993	Marie Claire (France)	1. China Times News Group 2. Nong-nong Magazine, Inc. (since 2000)	1. Licensee (1993–2000) 2. Joint venture (since 2000)

Table 4.2
Largest Women's Magazines in Taiwan, by Advertising Revenue, 2003

RANK	MAGAZINE	AD REVENUE (NT$ millions)	2003 PRINT RUN (thousands)
1	Vogue	190.4	600
2	Elle	190	660
3	Marie Claire	162	660
4	Nong-nong	108	660
5	Sugar	88	1800
6	Beauty (young)	84	3000

Source: Brain 338, 2004:6

Notes:

1. Excludes women's magazines with advertising revenue below NT$ 10 million
2. No complete tabulation of magazine circulation exists for Taiwan; an Audit Bureau of Circulation system has not yet been established.

Table 4.3.
Characteristics of the Readership of Leading Women's Magazines in Taiwan

READERSHIP (%)	NONG-NONG	BEAUTY	COSMOPOLITAN	ELLE	MARIE CLAIRE
Gender					
Female	90	–	77.8	96	97
Male	10	–	22.2	4	3
Age					
Under 20	10	–	0.7	14	2
21–25	35	85.8+	27.6	28	31
26–30	29	–	35	28	32
31–34	20	–	19.1	23	20
Above 35	6	–	17.6	14	15
Education					
Primary School	0	–	0	0	1+
Junior High	16+	–	0.9	2	–
Senior High	–	96+	44.5	29	28
Undergraduate	73	–	49.2	64	64
Graduate	11	–	5.4	5	7
Marital Status					
Married	80	–	23.6	35	34
Single	20	88.3	76.4	64	64
Others	0	–	0	0	2

Table 4.3.
Characteristics of the Readership of Leading Women's Magazines in Taiwan (continued)

Career					
Student	14	25	3.4	15	16
Homemaker	17	—	17.5	9	9
Civil Servant & Teacher	—	69+	8.7	—	—
Commerce, Finance, & Service	66	—	41.9	54	53
Professional	—	—	5.1	9	19
Others	3	—	23.4	—	3
Income					
20,001–30,000	—	46.7	28.8	—	—
30,001–40,000	25	29.1+	26	—	44+
40,001–50,000	11	—	15.7	—	—
Above 50,001	15	—	21	—	35
Living Place					
North	46	—	52.1	51	57
Central	27	—	30.6	20	17
South	23	—	12.7	26	21
East	4	—	3.8	3	4
Others	0	—	0.8	0	1

Notes:
1. "—" not available. "+": includes the next range.
2. Data provided by respective magazines.

Table 4.4.
Advertisements in Women's Magazines in Taiwan, 2003 (n)

	BEAUTY		NONG-NONG		COSMOPOLITAN		ELLE	
Total Pages	228		606		638		896	
Ad Pages	30.26%	(69)	40.26%	(244)	24.92%	(159)	43.97%	(394)
Product Origins								
Domestic	11.63%	(5)	18.82%	(32)	19.51%	(24)	8.09%	(22)
Transnational	88.37%	(38)	80.09%	(137)	78.86%	(97)	90.44%	(246)
Joint Venture	0%	(0)	0.59%	(1)	1.63%	(2)	1.47%	(4)
Total	100%	(43)	99.50%	(170)	100%	(123)	100%	(272)
Product Categories								
Beauty, Personal Products	83.72%	(36)	67.06%	(114)	55.28%	(68)	40.44%	(110)
Clothing and Accessories	0%	(0)	11.18%	(19)	28.46%	(35)	45.96%	(125)
Food & Beverages	4.65%	(2)	10.00%	(17)	8.94%	(11)	4.04%	(11)
Fitness	2.33%	(1)	2.35%	(4)	1.63%	(2)	0.37%	(1)
Home Appliances and Electronics	0%	(0)	2.35%	(4)	0.81%	(1)	1.47%	(4)
Books and Magazines	9.30%	(4)	2.94%	(5)	0.81%	(1)	1.10%	(3)
Others	0%	(0)	4.12%	(7)	4.07%	(5)	6.62%	(18)
Total	100.00%	(43)	100.00%	(170)	100.00%	(123)	100.00%	(272)

Table 4.5.
Product Category and Origin in Women's Magazine Advertisements in Taiwan (n)

PRODUCT ORIGIN[1]	BEAUTY & PERSONAL PRODUCTS		CLOTHING & ACCESSORIES		FOOD AND BEVERAGES		OTHERS[2]	
Domestic	25.3%	(83)	0		0		0	
Transnational	74.7%	(245)	100.0%	(179)	100.0%	(41)	100.0%	(53)
Total	100.0%	(328)	100.0%	(179)	100.0%	(41)	100.0%	(53)

Notes:
1. "Joint venture" excluded because of low incidence
2. "Foods and beverages," "fitness," "home appliances and electronics," and "books and magazines" categories combined with "others."

REFERENCES

100 leading media companies. (1998, August 17). *Advertising Age.*

Bagdikian, B. (1989, June 12). The lords of the global village, *The Nation*, pp. 805–820.

Bagdikian, B. (1992). *The media monopoly* (4th ed.). Boston: Beacon.

Bagdikian, B. (2000). *the media monopoly* (6th ed.). Boston: Beacon.

Barrell, J., & Braithwaite, B. (1988). *The business of women's magazines.* London: Kogan Page.

CNP Group merged Hua-Shie Cultural Enterprise. (1996, April 17). *Center Daily Times* (foreign edition in Chinese), p. 7.

Compaine, B. M. (1982). Magazines. In B. M., Compaine, C. H Sterling, T. Guback, & J. K. Noble Jr. (Eds.), *Who owns the media? Concentration of ownership in the mass communications industry* (pp. 143–187). White Plains, NY: Knowledge Industry Publications.

Damon-Moore, H., & Keastle C. F. (1991). Gender, advertising, and mass-circulation magazines. In C. F. Keastle et al. (Eds.), *Literacy in the United States* (pp. 245–271). New Haven, CT: Yale University Press.

Driver, S., & Gillespie, A. (1993). Structural change in the cultural industries: British magazine publishing in the 1980s. *Media, Culture and Society, 15,* 183–201.

Earnshaw, S. (1984). Advertising and the media: The case of women's magazines. *Media, Culture and Society, 6,* 411–421.

Elle is founded in October. (1991). *Brain, 178,* 48–49 (in Chinese).

Frith, K.T., & Tsao, J. (1998). Advertising and culture China: Challenges and opportunities in Asia. *Asian Journal of Communication, 8*(2), 8–17.

Gershon, R. A. (1993, Summer) International deregulation and the rise of transnational media corporations. *Journal of Media Economics,* 3–22.

Goldstein, C. (1989, June 29). The selling of Asia. *Far Eastern Economic Review, 144*(26), 61–63.

Hachette says half its earnings come from outside France. (1989, August 11). *Publishers Weekly,* p. 335.

Hayashi, R. (1995). Helping!?: Images and control in Japanese women's magazines. *Women's Studies in Communication, 18*(2), 189–198.

Hu, G. S. (1998). Entry and performance of transnational advertising agencies in Taiwan. *Asian Journal of Communication, 8*(2), 100–123.

Janus, N. Z. (1981). Advertising and the mass media in the era of the global corporation. In E. McAnany, J. Schnitman, & N. Janus (Eds.), *Communication and social structure—critical studies in mass media research* (pp. 287–316). New York: Praeger.

Ledbetter, J. (1996, January 16). Merge overkill. *Village Voice,* pp. 30–35.

Mattelart, A. (1991). *Advertising international: The privatization of public space.* New York: Routledge.

McCracken, E. (1983). In search of the female consumer: Latin American women's magazines and the transnational model. *Studies in Latin American Popular Culture, 2,* 226–233.

McCracken, E. (1993). *Decoding women's magazines: From* Mademoiselle *to* Ms. New York: St. Martin's.

Nong-nong (1994, July). Readers' report.

Shaw, P. (1997). *Demystifying women's magazines in Taiwan.* Unpublished doctoral dissertation, The Pennsylvania State University, State College, PA.

Shaw, P. (1999). The internationalization of the women's magazine industry in Taiwan: Context, process, and influence. *Asian Journal of Communication, 9*(2), 17–38.

Shaw, P. (2000). Changes in female roles in Taiwanese women's magazines, 1970–1994. *Media History, 6*(2), 151–160.

Shaw, P., & Wu, P. (2004). *Learning to be a woman—A content analysis of advertising in young women's magazines.* Unpublished working paper. Authors.

Smythe, D. (1981). *Dependency road: Communications, capitalism, consciousness, and Canada.* Norwood, NJ: Ablex.

The beautiful start of *Marie Claire.* (1993). *Brain, 202,* 42–44 (in Chinese).

The joint-ventured *Elle* magazine will be broken up. (1995). Collaboration and modernization: Case-study of a transnational magazine. *Studies in Latin American Popular Culture, 2,* 24–35.

Zomosa, A.L. (1983). Collaboration and modernization: Case-study of a transnational magazine. *Studies in Latin American Popular Culture, 2,* 24–35.

5

COMMERCIALIZING BEAUTY

A Comparison of Global and Local Magazine Advertising in Singapore

Katherine T. Frith

Advertising offers a unique opportunity to study how the beauty ideal is constructed across cultures. Because beauty is a construct that varies from culture to culture and changes over time, the idealization of beauty also shifts according to time and place. The beauty ideal in the United States in the 1950s, a buxom Marilyn Monroe, was soon to be replaced by the emaciated Twiggy of the 1960s. Whereas porcelain skin is valued in China, scarification of the skin is a beauty process in parts of Africa. Thus, the particular set of physical characteristics perceived as beautiful and desirable varies across cultures and over time. Advertisements offer us the opportunity to study the construction of beauty in a culture at a specific time because advertisers are notorious for promoting "a beauty ideal" (Greer, 1999) or, as Cortese (1999) points out, ads present "the exemplary female prototype." Given the current global expansion of the beauty industries across borders, it is surprising that there has not been more research on how women are depicted internationally in fashion and beauty magazines.

Singapore is an interesting country to study because it is both an Asian society and, at the same time, it is a very globalized society. In fact, Singapore received an award from *Foreign Policy* magazine in 2000 for being the "most globalized" country in the world. In terms of living standards and levels of development, Singapore is a developed country comparable to the United

States or a country in Western Europe. Although English is Singapore's official language, the population is approximately 70% Chinese and Mandarin is widely spoken. The influence of Confucianism is also quite strong in Singapore society. Like the other predominately Chinese societies in Asia, Confucian principles structure Singapore culture, creating a well-ordered society from the top down. In the Confucian tradition, certain relationships are accorded paramount importance. The Five Cardinal Relations (*wu lun*) are namely, "those between ruler and subject, father and son, elder brother and younger brother, husband and wife, and friend and friend" (Bond, 1986, p. 215). In each case, the senior member is accorded a wide range of prerogatives and authority with respect to the junior. Thus, although the rights of women in Singapore society are enviable to many women across Asia, there are still strong patriarchal influences and constraints on women's role in society. How these contrasting values are expressed in the representation of women in the media in Singapore is of interest, as traditional roles and modern roles are both at play in Singapore at this juncture in time.

As a modern, globalized city, Singapore is now host to a wide variety of international media. Special country editions of women's magazine titles such as *Elle, Cosmopolitan*, and *Harper's Bazaar* are now published each month in special Singapore editions. In this chapter, I compare the portrayals of women in advertising in the fashion and beauty magazines sold in Singapore with the intention of identifying the the ways advertising in global media and local media construct concepts of feminine beauty. This comparison of the advertising in local and global issues of women's magazines published in Singapore may help us see not only how women are portrayed in Singapore, but also what the future holds for images of women in the commercial media as other countries in Asia open their doors to the global media.

THEORETICAL ISSUES

Previous researchers have noted that women's magazines can act as agents of socialization, perpetuating certain gender stereotypes and global beauty standards such as thinness, and institutionalizing conventions such as photographic poses (Griffin, Viswanath, & Schwartz, 1994; Rudman & Verdi, 1993). Yet, little if any research has been done on how portrayals of women in global media might differ from those in local media. Specifically, the question I address in this chapter is: How is feminine beauty constructed in the advertising found in global and local women's magazines in Singapore?

Globalization theory holds that increased trade and improved communication technologies are bringing about increasing levels of global integration between cultures (Giddens, 1990; Thompson, 1997). Although women's magazines have long been identified as a socializing force in many women's lives, until relatively recently, the most popular women's magazines in most countries were locally produced. Starting in the 1990s, this changed as global media began to publish local editions in many countries. With the rise of international media corporations and the spread of international editions of women's magazines, "best practices" in things such as photographic conventions and content areas are being rapidly disseminated around the globe (Shaw, 1999). However, there is a paucity of research comparing how advertisers in global and local magazines in a given society construct beauty.

Global Media

The internationalization of women's magazines is not a new phenomenon. *Harper's Bazaar*, a U.S. magazine, began publishing a U.K. edition as early as 1929 (Hafstrand, 1995) and *Elle*, a European-based women's magazine, expanded into Japan in the late 1960s. However as Herman and McChesney (1997) note, "the establishment of an integrated global media market only began in earnest in the late 1980s and did not reach its full potential until the 1990s" (p. 10). If we look at *Elle* magazine, owned by the French publishing giant Hachette Filipacchi, we can see that in terms of international expansion the last twenty years have been the most aggressive (see Appendix B, Table 5.1).

Hachette Filipacchi first launched *Elle* in 1945 and it now prints 36 special country editions—including editions in the local languages of India, Thailand, China, and Korea—selling more than 60 million copies a year. It was the first international fashion monthly on newsstands in China when it launched there in 1988, and it has a presence in most countries in the Asian region.

Like other global media, magazines use several different strategies to enter foreign markets, and these range from exporting, licensing, and joint ventures to setting up wholly owned subsidiaries. The simplest way for a magazine to enter a foreign market is to export; that is, to manufacture the magazine in the home country and export it, unchanged, to foreign markets. Hafstrand notes that Sweden imports over 700 different titles, about 90% of them from Great Britain, the United States, and Germany (Hafstrand, 1995).

In a licensing agreement, a foreign magazine company will allow a local publisher to use its brand name and editorial strategies for a fee or royalties. The local publisher then creates a national edition of the foreign magazine. *Cosmopolitan,* available in over 30 countries worldwide, mainly publishes under licensing agreements, as does the magazine *Marie Claire.*

A joint venture involves the shared ownership of a magazine edition. This can range anywhere from a 50–50 proposition to a combination in which one partner is a virtually silent participant. Joint ventures involve a

higher level of commitment than licensing. *Elle* operates fully owned subsidiaries in Spain and Greece, but to enter the highly competitive German
and U.K. markets, the company formed joint ventures with strong domestic partners (Hafstrand, 1995). In Singapore, as in most other Asian countries, the government has strict regulations on the ownership of media,
requiring the international editions of women's magazines to form joint ventures with local publishing partners (Reilly, 1998).

The driving force behind internationalization is the saturation of home
markets. While the United States, for example, has been losing women's
titles due to heavy saturation of the market (Condé Nast recently closed
down *Mademoiselle* due to competition and flagging sales), markets with
high economic growth rates, for example, Asian countries such as China,
Singapore, and Korea, have become important targets for Western publishers of women's fashion and beauty magazines.

A second reason for expanding the reach of these international magazines is to generate revenue by providing international consumer brands
with advertising vehicles that reach into these expanding foreign markets. A
company such as Chanel, for example, can make a deal with Hachette (own-
ers of *Elle* magazine) to run a global campaign translated into many languages in 35 of Hachette's magazines in the United States, Europe, South
America, and Asia. Demand is high for advertising space in media that offer
a consistent look and feel across borders.

Ideally, for advertising messages to be resonant with a target audience
they need to reflect the social norms of the specific society in which the ads
appear. In a perfect world, advertisements would be created by members of
a particular society and consumed by members of the same society.
However, as Bagdikian (1992) argues, in the new global system that inte-
grates worldwide mass media with worldwide mass advertising, the large
publishing groups have consolidated their control over magazine markets.
Many women's magazines appearing in Asia now, such as *Vogue, Elle,* and
Cosmopolitan, are part of larger media conglomerates such as Bertelsmann,
Time Warner, Hearst, Hachette Filipacchi, and Condé Nast.

The international versions of these global magazines differ from the
"local" women's magazines in that the international ones tend to carry a pre-
ponderance of advertisements for transnational products (Shaw, 1999). The
popularity of these international magazines is growing in most parts of Asia,
and the introduction of these magazines has brought in certain Western
advertising conventions. In a study comparing images of women in weekly
U.S. news magazines (*Time* and *Life*) to weekly Indian magazines (*India
Today* and *Illustrated Weekly of India*), Griffin, Viswanath, and Schwartz
(1994) found that many of the Western advertising conventions and poses
for women were being transferred across cultures. They reported that female
models in India were adopting poses and displays that conformed closely to

gender portrayals in the advertising of the industrialized Western nations. Most recently, Frith, Shaw, and Cheng (2005) analyzed advertisements from local women's fashion and beauty magazines in Singapore, Taiwan, and the United States. They compared the ways in which Caucasian and Asian models were portrayed in print advertisements in those countries and found that Caucasian models were shown more frequently in seductive dress.

Finally, an economic concern that has been voiced recently in some Asian countries is that international magazines are having an impact on the local magazine industry. For example, in Malaysia, the increasing encroachment by foreign magazines is diverting readers and advertisers away from local publications. Although international magazine titles account for only 10% of the magazines available in the local Malaysian market, they command about 60% of the total advertising spending in the magazine category and reach mainly up-market consumer readers (Singh, 2003). In China, the magazine advertising market is growing at 37% annually with total revenue of U.S. $5.5 billion in 2003 (Roberts, 2003). Many of the international women's magazines have established Mandarin editions for the Chinese market and are competing with local Chinese magazines for market share.

The Feminist Critique

Advertising has long been criticized by Western feminist scholars as a pervasive cultural institution that represents women in a problematic and often unacceptable way (Kates, Shaw, & Garlock, 1999). In particular, the positioning of women as sexual objects in ads has received a great deal of discussion (Jhally, 1989; Kilbourne, 1999). Although numerous U.S. studies have suggested that sexual content interferes with brand name recall (Alexander & Judd, 1978; Chestnut, LaChance, & Lubitz, 1977; Horton, Lieb, & Hewitt, 1982; Richmond & Hartman, 1982; Steadman, 1969), nonetheless attractive female bodies and sexual stimuli have historically been used in the United States to grab the viewer's attention and attempt to lend interest to a product or service (Frith & Mueller, 2003; Lafky, Duffy, Steinways, & Berkowitz, 1996). According to Reichert, Lambiase, Carstarphen, and Zavoina (1999):

> In *TV Guide*, more than 35 percent of network promotional ads contain some sort of sexual reference. An analysis of Clio award-winning TV spots revealed that 29 percent contained a seductively dressed model, and 27 percent contained at least a hint of sexual suggestion. (p. 7)

The literature on sex appeal in advertising is extensive. Soley and Kurzbad (1986) compared "sex appeals" in magazine ads in the United States between

1964 and 1984. They found that, over time, sexual elements were becoming more visual and more overt. They concluded that female nudity and erotic content had become quite commonplace in contemporary U.S. ads. Another study of women's magazines from 1983 to 1993 showed increasing representation of women as sexual objects (Reichert et al., 1999). Reid and Soley (1983) found that ads with sexual content got higher visual recall/recognition scores, but the same did not apply to the verbal content.

Although there have been fewer studies comparing representation of women across cultures, Griffin, Viswanath, and Schwartz (1994) compared images of women in weekly U.S. news magazines to weekly Indian magazines and found the use of "sexual pursuit" as a theme in advertisements (men pursuing women in an overtly sexual way) was used three times more often in U.S. magazines than in Indian magazines. Frith and Mueller (2003) noted that in conservative Asian countries such as Malaysia and Indonesia only Caucasian women were used in lingerie advertising, as showing partially undressed local women was not acceptable to local cultural norms.

Globalization and the Construction of Beauty

The beauty industries are booming in Asia. In 2003, Chinese women alone bought over US$9 billion worth of beauty products (Harney, 2005). This beauty bonanza has developed because millions of affluent professional Asian women have entered the 21st century as a strong economic force (Naisbitt, 1996). Many Asian women are well educated, business-minded and are determined to succeed in a male dominated world. In China, women already made up 25% of all entrepreneurs, about 20% of all management jobs in Hong Kong were held by women, and the number of female managers in Singapore had tripled over the previous few decades (Naisbitt, 1996). In Asia, one way women believe they can succeed is through beauty. Data from *The Real Truth about Beauty: A Global Report* (Dove, 2004) showed women's evaluation of the importance of beauty to the external society, and the findings are very interesting. When asked whether "physically attractive women are more valued by men," a majority of women in Asia agreed. In Singapore, 68% of women surveyed felt this was an important factor. When asked whether "beautiful women have greater opportunities in life," an overwhelming 75% of Singaporean women strongly agreed (Dove, 2004).

Beauty pageants have become big business in countries such as Singapore. In fact, parents of children as young as 8 years old are spending thousands of dollars on performance classes so their children can participate in pageants such as Little Miss Singapore World, Little Miss Singapore Universe, and the Disney-sponsored, Disney Princess Pageant (Chee, 2005).

Manufacturers of beauty products are thrilled with the burgeoning interest in beauty in this region, and advertisers are spending millions of dollars to sell their products to women in Singapore and throughout Asia.

Ideally, for advertising messages to be resonant with a target audience, marketing theory holds that ads would need to reflect the social norms and cultural values of a given society (Belk, Bryce, & Pollay, 1985; Belk & Pollay, 1985; Cheng, 1994, 1997; Frith & Sengupta, 1991; Lin, 1993; Mueller, 1987). In a perfect world, we might expect advertisements to be created by members of a particular society and consumed by members of the same society. However, globalization alters this process. Standardized campaigns can be created in the head offices of advertising agencies in the United States and Europe and run in foreign countries with only simple modifications such as translated headlines. The result is that the forms of representation, particularly of women, can take on a globalized or transnational look. As one Korean author put this:

> For thirty years, media have been taken to task for reproducing and reinforcing stereotyped images of women. Yet unfair representations of women in media still prevail worldwide. Sex stereotyping has been so deeply ingrained, even glorified, that the women themselves have become desensitized to their own inferior portrayal. The prospects appear even gloomier as the globalization of media progresses. (Kyung-Ja Lee, 2000, p. 86)

To better understand how beauty is represented in magazine advertising, this study builds on previous research by Solomon, Ashmore, and Longo (1992) and Englis, Solomon, and Ashmore (1994). In the 1990s, these researchers conducted an experiment in which they assembled a set of photographs of models employed by major U.S. fashion agencies and presented them to a sample of U.S. fashion magazine editors who were instructed to sort the models into piles based on similarity of looks. The results yielded relatively distinct beauty types: Classic, Feminine, Sensual, Exotic, Cute, Girl-Next-Door, Sex Kitten, and Trendy.

In order to test the reliability of these categories in a Singaporean context, Siew, Ching, and Tan (2001) interviewed local fashion magazine editors and advertising art directors in Singapore and conducted a content analysis of five years worth of Singaporean women's magazines (1996 to 2000). These researchers found that although the U.S. categories were viable in Singapore, one category, "exotic," was irrelevant as it was defined by Englis et al. (1994) as "non-Caucasian." Thus, this category was excluded from the present study. Siew, Ching, and Tan also found that some of the other categories, such as Classic and Feminine, and Cute and Girl-Next-Door, shared many general characteristics and thus these categories were combined for the purpose of this study into Classic and Cute. In fact, the Cute category was also identified as a viable beauty type in Asia in a study on Japan by researchers. In comparing the beauty types of young girls in a Japanese version of *Seventeen* magazine to a U.S. issue of the same magazine, the researchers reported that the Japanese models were typecast as "cute" and "girlish" (smiling and giggling) more often, whereas the American girls were posed with more serious expressions, looking more defiant and independent (Maynard & Taylor, 1999).

Finally, Siew, Ching, and Tan (2001) noted that in their research, the categories identified by Englis, Solomon, and Ashmore (1994) as Sensual and Sex Kitten overlapped, and so they were combined into one category, Sexy. As a result, the coding categories for beauty types in this study were: Classic, Sexy, Cute, and Trendy. (See operational definitions for these categories in Appendix A, Figures 5.1 to 5.3.)

Method

Based on the literature review, advertisements from popular fashion and beauty women's magazines available in Singapore were content analyzed for the ethnicity of model, product category, and beauty type (see Appendix A for operational definitions of categories). Singapore is a culturally diverse Asian country with the Chinese making up about 70% of the population, followed by about 20% Malays and 9% Indians (Caucasians make up about 1% of the population).

According to Wimmer and Dominick (2000), content analysis can aid in comparing media content to the real world. In this case, content analysis allows us to examine the portrayal of feminine beauty in global and local magazines. In addition to beauty types, the product category and the ethnicity of the models were analyzed. Whereas, Cortese (1999) contends that advertisers present the exemplary female prototype in advertising, regardless of product or service, other researchers (Cheng & Schweitzer, 1996; Mueller, 1987) have found a relationship between product categories and cultural values. Mueller (1987) argues that in cross-cultural research it is essential to observe the relationship between the product advertised and the appeal being made to the consumer; thus, I included product categories in this analysis.

To maintain comparability, the two most popular local women's magazines, *Her World* and *Female,* were compared to the Singapore editions of the two most popular global women's magazines, *Harper's Bazaar* and *Elle.* In terms of circulation figures, *Female* is the second best selling magazine in Singapore after *Her World*. Although global women's magazines rank much lower in terms of overall circulation figures compared to local magazines, *Harper's Bazaar* and *Elle* are among the most popular and influential

Singapore editions of global women's magazines. All of the magazines in this study are published in English, the main local language.

For the purpose of this study, three issues of each magazine were chosen at random from within the 14-month period from March 2000 to April 2003. The unit of analysis was restricted to advertisements of one or more full pages, containing at least one woman. The coding criteria for beauty types required that both the face and some part of the model's dress be shown in the ad. In advertisements where more than one woman was present, the largest or most dominant woman was coded. Advertisements with numerous representations of women of the same size, or having no dominant main character, were not included in the collection. Identical advertisements were included in the coding process because repetition is a strategy frequently used in advertising campaigns. As a result, a total of 771 advertisements were collected from the above-mentioned women's fashion and beauty magazines.

Three research questions guided this study:

R1: What is the ethnicity of the models shown in global women's magazines and local women's magazines in Singapore?

R2: Will the beauty types used in global women's magazines differ from the beauty types used in local women's magazines in Singapore?

R3: Will the types of products advertised in global women's magazines differ from those in local women's magazines in Singapore.

Coding

Two independent, bilingual (speaking both English and Mandarin) Singaporean coders analyzed the advertisements. Coders were trained using a preliminary subset of about 50 advertisements. The coders met to compare their results (Holsti, 1969). When disagreements arose, coders discussed their interpretations and a final decision was made by consensus. This process continued until both coders were comfortable with the categories. Definitions and examples of the various categories were available at all times. Intercoder reliability was at least 86% agreement for each category.

Findings

As shown in Table 5.2 (Appendix B), Caucasian models far outnumbered local models in advertisements in *all* publications. In *Her World* and *Female*, 72% of the models shown were Caucasian and only about 25% were local

(Caucasians make up only about 1% of the population in Singapore). In the global women's magazines 90% of all models used were Caucasian.

In terms of the beauty types of models shown in ads in all Singapore women's magazines, the Classic Beauty type far out numbered the other types (see Appendix B, Table 5.3). In local magazines, 74% of all the models shown were Classic beauties, whereas in the global media 69% of women shown were of this beauty type.

Interestingly, when the sample is analyzed for ethnicity of model by beauty type we can see that the figures in Table 5.4 (Appendix B) might be misleading. In fact, when Chinese models are used in ads they are shown as Classic beauties 80% of the time and Chinese models are used in Sexy poses only 3% of the time. Caucasian models were depicted as Classic beauties only 71% of the time and were used far more than Chinese models in sexually suggestive poses (16%).

One of the most interesting findings of this study supported the finding of earlier research by Frith, Shaw, and Cheng (2005) that unlike the U.S. women's magazines, women's magazines in Asia featured a greater proportion of ads for beauty products than clothing. This finding also applies to the current study. In comparing local women's magazines in Singapore with global magazines I found that beauty products made up about 45% of all ads in the local magazines followed by clothing (36%). In global magazines clothing accounted for over 50% of all the advertisements (see Appendix B, Table 5.5).

Discussion

The purpose of this research was to compare the construction of beauty in advertising in global and local women's magazines published in Singapore to try and understand the impact of globalization on the construction of female beauty. Overall, the predominant ethnic group used for female models in both local and global magazines was Caucasians. The Classic beauty type was also the predominant beauty type used in both types of magazines. However, when the ethnicity of models was examined, it was found that 80% of the time Chinese models are shown in a Classic beauty type, whereas Caucasians were used this way only about 70% of the time. Interestingly, Caucasian women are being presented in sexual poses (16%) far more often than are Chinese models (3%).

In other words, the advertising adage that "sex sells" seems to apply more to Caucasians than Asian models. This may be related to traditional artistic representations of Asian women in art history. As Berger (1972) and Shields (1990) have noted, there has been a tradition in Western art of displaying the female body. However, this has not been the tradition in Chinese or Malay art (the two predominant ethnic groups in Singapore). Historically, when women appear in traditional Chinese paintings they are often clothed in loose robes, and the face and hair rather than the body become the central focus. In Malay art, because of the influence of Islam, women are always depicted in modest dress and pose. Thus, traditions of "gaze" may very well have developed differently in Singapore and this may be reflected in the way local models are portrayed in terms of beauty in advertising.

The finding that product categories differed significantly between local and global women's magazines further supports this contention. Beauty products aimed at improving women's hair, skin, and face occupied the greatest proportion of ads in local Singaporean magazines (45%). The percentage of beauty products advertised in global women's magazines was much lower (25%). Clothing ads occupied the largest proportion of ads in the global magazines (53%). Thus, advertising in global women's magazines calls attention to the body of the model (because clothing ads show more of the model's figure than ads for skin and hair products). Clothing has traditionally been related to the body. Wood (1999) explains that clothing is designed to call attention to women's bodies, as clothing makes women more "attractive to viewers" (p. 145). The high proportion of clothing ads in global women's magazines, coupled with the higher proportion of the Sexy beauty type (used with Caucasian women) suggests that there are differences in the way women of differing ethnicities are being constructed in terms of beauty in advertising in Singapore.

One might also wonder why there is such a high percentage of Caucasian models being used in advertisements in this Asian country. Although globalization might be one possible answer, nonetheless, the overuse of white models may create unfair expectations in Singaporean women by holding up an unattainable beauty ideal. In fact, the fixation with "skin whitening" products in Singapore may be in response to this overuse of white models. Advertisers have a history of exploiting women's insecurities, and although porcelain skin has been a traditional signifier of Chinese beauty, nonetheless, the overuse of white models in Singaporean advertising might contribute to the increasing sales of products such as whitening creams in this country.

As global media grow in popularity and begin to take readers away from the local media in countries like Singapore, it would be advantageous for researchers to question the impact of imported beauty ideals on local audiences. It might also be advantageous for local women's groups to question whether globalization justifies the overuse of ethnic models who are not widely represented in the populations of the country. When the predominant models shown in ads in a country such as Singapore are of an ethnic group that does not represent local beauty, the advertisers are reifying beauty standards that are unattainable to local audiences. So even with the purchase of more and more expensive beauty treatments and products, local audiences cannot achieve "the look" being featured in these women's magazines.

Finally, as global women's magazines gain circulation in Asian markets women in other countries might study the impact of globalization on women's magazines in Singapore. Although it certainly makes economic sense from the multinational advertiser's point of view to create one global campaign in New York or London featuring a Caucasian model and then run the campaign worldwide in magazines such as *Elle* or *Harper's,* it makes less sense from the point of view of protecting local cultures and identity. Thus, globalization of women's magazines has pluses and minuses in regard to local audiences in Asia.

APPENDIX A

Chinese	This racial type included all Chinese women.
Caucasian	This included Caucasians, Hispanics, and Europeans.
Other Asian	This included all other Asian models such as Indian, Malay, Eurasian, etc.
Other	This included African models or models whose ethnicity could not be easily determined.

Figure 5.1. Operationalizations of Race/Ethnic Types Examined in Women's Magazine Ads

Classic	Slightly older than average, the model has an elegant feminine look. With fair skin and a glamorous and sophisticated look, she usually wears soft, feminine, but not heavily accessorized apparel.
Sexy	The model is posed in a sexually attractive way. She usually wears sexy attire or tight-fitting, revealing clothes.
Cute	With casual attire, the model has a cute and youthful appearance. She can also be outdoorsy, in a casual, active manner.
Trendy	The model usually wears faddish clothes, and displays oversized accessories. Her hair is tousled. There is a slight sense of chaos to this type. She can also have an "I-don't-give-a-damn" attitude.

Figure 5.2. Operationalizations of Beauty Types Examined in Women's Magazine Ads

Beauty	All cosmetics, hair care products, and skin care products.
Clothing	All clothing designers and manufacturers.
Accessories	Sunglasses, scarves, purses, shoes, hand phones, and other accessories.
Other	This category includes all other products.

Figure 5.3. Product Categories Examined in Women's Magazine Ads

APPENDIX B

Table 5.1
The Internationalization of Elle

YEAR	COUNTRY
1969	Japan
1985	Great Britain, United States
1986	Spain
1987	Hong Kong, Italy
1988	Brazil, Greece, China, Portugal, Sweden, Germany
1989	The Netherlands, Quebec
1990s	Australia, Taiwan
1991–2003	Singapore, Korea, Czech Republic, Thailand, China, Russia, Croatia, plus 13 other countries

Table 5.2
Ethnicity of Models in Women's Magazine Ads
in Singapore

MAGAZINES	LOCAL		GLOBAL		TOTAL	
Ethnicity	N	%	N	%	N	%
Chinese	120	22	16	7	136	17
Caucasian	392	72	224	90	616	78
Other Asian	14	3	1	1	15	2
African	14	3	6	2	20	3

Table 5.3
Beauty Types of Models in Women's Magazine Ads in Singapore

MAGAZINES	LOCAL		GLOBAL		TOTAL	
BEAUTY	N	%	N	%	N	%
CLASSIC	394	74	165	69	559	73
SEXY	62	12	40	17	102	13
CUTE	56	10	20	8	76	10
TRENDY	19	4	15	6	34	4
TOTAL	531	100	240	100	771	100

Table 5.4
Ethnicity of Models in Women's Magazine Ads in Singapore, by Beauty Type

BEAUTY TYPE	CLASSIC		SEXUAL		CUTE		TRENDY		TOTAL	
ETHNICITY	N	%	N	%	N	%	N	%	N	%
CHINESE	106	80	4	3	22	17	0	0	132	100
CAUCASIAN	427	71	98	16	48	8	31	5	604	100
OTHER ASIAN	9	60	0	0	6	40	0	0	15	100
OTHER	17	85	0	0	0	0	3	15	20	100
TOTAL	559	102	76	34	771	100				

Table 5.5
Beauty Types of Models in Women's Magazine Ads in Singapore, by Products Advertised

MAGAZINES	LOCAL		GLOBAL		TOTAL	
PRODUCTS	N	%	N	%	N	%
BEAUTY	236	45	61	25	297	39
CLOTHING	193	36	127	53	310	40
FOOD/DRINK	5	1	4	2	9	1
ACCESSORIES	63	12	45	19	108	14
OTHER	34	6	3	1	47	6
TOTAL	531	100	240	100	771	100

REFERENCES

Alexander, W., & Judd, B. (1978). Do nudes in ads enhance brand recall? *Journal of Advertising Research, 18*, 47–50.

Bagdikian, B. H. (1992). *The media monopoly* (5th ed.). Boston: Beacon.

Belk, R., & Pollay, R. (1985). Materialism and status appeal in Japanese and U.S. print advertising: A historical and cross cultural content analysis. *International Marketing Review, 2*(12), 38–47.

Belk, R. W., Bryce, W., & Pollay, R. (1985). Materialism and individual determinism in U.S. and Japanese television advertising. In R. Lutz (Ed.), *Advances in consumer research* (pp. 568–572). Provo, UT: Association for Consumer Research.

Berger, J. (1972). *Ways of seeing.* London: Penguin.

Bond, M. (1986). *The psychology of the Chinese people.* London: Oxford University Press.

Chee, F. (2005, November 6) Twinkle, twinkle little star. *Straits Times*, p. L2.

Cheng, H. (1994). Reflections of cultural values: A content analysis of Chinese magazine advertisements from 1982 and 1992. *International Journal of Advertising, 13*, 167–183.

Cheng, H. (1997). Holding up half of the sky: A sociocultural comparison of gender role portrayals in Chinese and U.S. advertising. *International Journal of Advertising, 16*, 295–319.

Cheng, H., & Schweitzer, J. C. (1996). Cultural values reflected in Chinese and U.S. television commercials. *Journal of Advertising Research, 36*, 27–45.

Chestnut, R., La Chance, C., & Lubitz, A. (1977). The decorative female model: Sexual stimuli and the recognition of advertisements. *Journal of Advertising, 6*, 11–14.

Cortese, A. J. (1999). *Provocateur: Images of women and minorities in advertising.* Lanham, MD: Rowman & Littlefield.

Dove (2004). *The real truth about beauty: A global report.* Retrieved November 6, 2005, from *www.campaignforrealbeauty.com/ uploadedfiles/dove_white_paper_final. pdf*

Englis, B., Solomon, M., & Ashmore, R. (1994). Beauty before the eyes of beholders: The cultural encoding of beauty types in magazine advertising and music television. *Journal of Advertising, 23*(2), 49–63.

Frith, K. T., & Mueller, B. (2003). *Advertising and societies: Global issues.* New York: Peter Lang.

Frith, K. T., & Sengupta, S. (1991). Individualism and advertising: A cross cultural comparison. *Media Asia, 18*, 191–197.

Frith, K. T., Shaw, P., & Cheng, H. (2005). The construction of beauty: A cross cultural analysis of women's magazine advertisements. *Journal of Communication, 55*(1), 56–70

Giddens, A. (1990). *The consequences of modernity.* Cambridge: Polity.

Greer, G. (1999). *The whole woman.* London: Doubleday.

Griffin, M., Viswanath, K., & Schwartz, D. (1994). Gender advertising in the U.S. and India: Exporting cultural stereotypes. *Media, Culture & Society, 16*, 487–507.

Hafstrand, H. (1995). Consumer magazines in transition: A study of approaches to internationalization. *The Journal of Media Economics, 8*(1), 1–12.

Harney, A. (2005, November 6). The china doll revolution. *The Financial Times*, p. W1.

Herman, E., & McChesney, R. (1997). *The global media: The new missionaries of corporate capitalism.* London: Cassell.

Holsti, O. R. (1969). *Content analysis for the social sciences and humanities.* Reading, MA: Addison-Wesley.

Horton, R., Lieb, L., & Hewitt, M. (1982). The effects of nudity, suggestiveness, and attractiveness on product class and brand name recall. In V. Kothari (Ed.), *Developments in marketing science* (Vol. 5, pp. 456–459). Nacogdoches, TX: Academy of Marketing Science.

Jhally, S. (1989). Advertising, gender and sex: What's wrong with a little objectification? In R. Parmentier & G. Urban (Eds.), *Working papers and the proceedings of the Center for Psychosocial Studies*, No. 29.

Kates, S., Shaw, G., & Garlock, G. (1999). The ever entangling web: A study of ideologies and discourses in advertising to women. *Journal of Advertising, 28*(2), 33–49.

Kilbourne, J. (1999). *Can't buy me love: How advertising changes the way we think and feel.* New York: Free Press.

Kyung-J. L. (2000). Country experiences: Korea. In J. Malipon (Ed.), *Changing lenses: Women's perspectives on media.* Manila: ISIS International.

Lafky, S., Duffy, M., Steinways, M., & Berkowitz, D. (1996). Looking through gendered lenses: Female stereotyping in advertisements and gender role expectations. *Journalism and Mass Communications Quarterly, 73*(2), 379–388.

Lin, C. A. (1993). Cultural differences in message strategies: A comparison between American and Japanese TV commercials. *Journal of Advertising Research, 33*(3), 40–48.

Maynard, M., & Taylor, C. (1999). Girlish images across cultures: Analyzing Japanese versus U.S. *Seventeen* magazine ads. *Journal of Advertising, 28*(1), 39–48.

Mueller, B. (1987). Reflections of culture: An analysis of Japanese and American advertising appeals. *Journal of Advertising Research, 27*(3), 51–59.

Naisbitt, J. (1996). *Megatrends Asia: Eight Asian megatrends are reshaping our world.* New York: Simon and Schuster.

Reichert, T., Lambiase, S., Carstarphen, M., & Zavoina, S. (1999). Cheesecake and beefcake: No matter how you slice it, sexual explicitness in advertising continues to increase. *Journalism and Mass Communications Quarterly, 76*(1), 7–20.

Reid, L. N., & Soley, L. (1983). Decorative models and the readership of magazine ads. *Journal of Advertising Research, 23*(2), 27–32.

Reilly, P. (1998, April 3). *Cosmo* to tone down language for version planned for China? Hearst is among the first from West to win right of publication since 1989. *Wall Street Journal*, p. B7.

Richmond, D., & Hartman, T. (1982). Sex appeal in advertising. *Journal of Advertising Research, 22*, 53–61.

Roberts, D. (2003, November 10). Foreign magazines are a hit in China. Will the party let them prosper? *Business Week*, (November 10): p. 20.

Rudman, W. J., & Verdi, P. (1993). Exploitation: Comparing sexual and violent imagery of females and males in advertising. *Women and Health, 20*(4), 1–14.

Shaw, P. (1999). Internationalization of the women's magazine industry in Taiwan: Context, process and influence. *Asian Journal of Communication, 9*(2), 17–38.

Shields, V. R. (1990). Advertising visual images: Gendered ways of seeing and looking. *Journal of Communication Inquiry, 14*(2), 25–39.

Siew, F., Ching, K. S., & Tan, W. K. (2001). *Colours of beauty: Selecting and using Pan Asian, Asian and Caucasian models in Singapore women's fashion magazines.* Unpublished honors thesis. Singapore: Nanyang Technological University.

Singh, B. (2003, July 1). Magazine publishers' body formed. *Malaysian Business,* Kuala Lumpur, p. 36.

Soley, L., & Kurzbad, G. (1986). Sex in advertising: A comparison of 1964 and 1984 magazine advertisements. *Journal of Advertising, 15*(3), 46–54, 64.

Solomon, M. R., Ashmore, R., & Longo, L. C. (1992). The beauty match-up hypothesis: Congruence between types of beauty and product images in advertising. *Journal of Advertising, 21*, 23–34.

Steadman, M. (1969). How sexy illustrations affect brand recall. *Journal of Advertising Research, 9*, 15–19.

Thompson, K. (1997). *Media and cultural regulation.* London: Sage.

Wimmer, R. D., & Dominick, J. (2000). *Mass media research: An introduction.* Belmont, CA: Wadsworth.

Wood, J. (1999). *Communication, gender and culture* (3rd ed.). Belmont, CA: Wadsworth.

6

VISUAL PORTRAYAL
OF WOMEN IN THE MEDIA

Modern Indian "Stereotypes"

Kavita Karan

The portrayal of women across cultures has been a subject of research, particularly in media and feminist studies for decades. Tracing the changes from the early 1950s to the present, women in the media have been molded into stereotypical roles, and although their portrayal has at times kept up with the social changes, women have often been marginalized into a secondary status and their bodies have been exploited (Ewen & Ewen, 1982; Ferguson, Kreshel, & Tinkham, 1990; Frith & Mueller, 2003; Geraghty, 2000; Miller, 1981). Society defines attributes of femininity and to a large extent these attributes, stereotypes and cultural icons are replicated in both print and broadcast media (Ahmed, 1998; Chang, Palasthira, & Kim, 1995; Choudhary, 1992; Dreze & Sen, 1996; Edwards & Roces, 2000; Ferguson et al., 1990; Frith & Mueller, 2003; Munshi, 2001; Prasad, 2005). Advertising has also mirrored these societal icons and at times perpetuated misconceptions and stereotypes about gender roles in society, despite the increasing awareness of feminist concerns (Butler, 1990; Ferguson et al., 1990; Mills, 1995).

Similar to most Asian countries, India has been a tradition-bound society, with clearly defined gender roles and value systems maintaining the superior status of men. Many women continue to be the victims of exploitation, social abuse, rape, and neglect. However, there is another side of the picture that is emerging. Global and local changes are redefining women's roles, and this is impacting on their representation and portrayal in the media. A minor revolution is taking place with the social, economic, and media forces attempting to bring about substantive change. These developments are empowering women to identify and project themselves as equal and active members of the society. Increased literacy, greater awareness through access and exposure to the media and information technologies, increased political participation and the increasingly powerful forces of the global economy are gradually reshaping the Indian woman of the twenty-first century (Anand, 1992; Desai & Patel, 1985; Ganguly-Scrase, 2000; Karan, 1990; Kumar, 1993; Mehta, 1997; Thakur, 1997). In the process of change, media is acting as a catalyst in spearheading this developmental process (Thakur, 1997). The increasing penetration of national and cable television in urban and rural households have increased the viewing time for Indian women. The print media have also diversified to cater to women's needs. The space devoted to women in Indian newspapers and magazines, in both English and Indian languages has increased to meet the diverse needs of women. Women's magazines, in English and regional languages, have become a source of information and enlightenment for many urban women. The winds of change are apparent in advertising. Bhagat (2003) found that Indian advertising has also changed to reflect the modern Indian women.

In this chapter, I present a view on the evolving portrayal of women in print advertisements. Based on the theoretical framework and content analysis of the classification of beauty types proposed by Solomon, Ashmore, and Longo (1992) and Englis, Solomon, and Ashmore (1994) and further refined for the Asian region by Frith, Cheng, and Shaw, (2004), I examine the images of beauty types displayed in Indian women's magazines. I also look at the ethnicity of models, the products they advertise, and the occupational roles represented to determine the dominant cultural issues. Some of the factors that have contributed to the concept of "Indian beauty" in the last decade and their representation in the media are also discussed. This is done with the understanding that advertising plays a number of roles in society. On the one hand, the role of the advertising agency is to position products to specific target audiences and design campaigns that would promote the product or service in a competitive market place. On the other hand, advertising often uses images that may affect the social and cultural environment within which they appear. Thus, in this chapter I examine many arguments from the literature without dismissing their merits or demerits.

THE STATUS OF INDIAN WOMEN—HISTORICAL PERSPECTIVES AND PRESENT TRENDS

The status of women in India continues to be much lower despite the fact that the country was led for over a decade by the late Prime Minister Mrs.

Indira Gandhi, one the most dynamic Asian leaders of the twentieth century. The status of Indian women can be studied from the mythological and historical perspectives to the more modern views. The mythological epics of the *Ramayana* and *Mahabharata* and the historical tales talk about the virtues of the ideal woman devoted to her husband, who would toil tirelessly for the household, attend to the needs of the family, and at some point in time, even depart from the world sitting on the funeral pyre of the husband (Kamat, 2003; Kumar, 1993; Mani, 1990; Rege, 1995; Sangari & Vaid, 1994). These tales from the mythological epics serialized on television continue to perpetuate the traditional and submissive woman's role and have consistently had high viewership and commanded the highest of advertising revenues (Bhatt, 1991; Joshi, 1991; Krishnan & Dighe, 1990).

Indian women are both revered and abused. Ironically, though religion encompasses the worship of womanhood by both men and women as evidenced by the goddesses Laxmi (the goddess of wealth), Parvati (the goddess of learning), and Kali (the goddess of power), women's power in the heavenly abode is not projected to women on earth (Hawley & Wulff, 1996), which is apparent in many ways.

India is the seventh largest country, and with over a billion people it is the second most populated country in the world. The low sex ratio, with 933 women for every 1,000 men is an indication of the neglect of female children, higher mortality rates, selective abortion, and female infanticide, all of which are indicators of the status of the women in the country. The birth of a daughter is still not an occasion to celebrate, as contrasted with that of a son. From childhood, women are trained to develop skills in housekeeping and in clearly defined roles, amply supported with illustrations in primary and middle school textbooks (Kalia, 1988). Despite several reforms, age-old social practices continue; marriages are still fixed by parents, most times even without the consent of the young girls. The dowry system[1] (Caplan, 1984; Sharma, 1985) continues to plague Indian women despite years of effort by government, nongovernmental bodies, and women activists to stop the practice.

After marriage, women are bonded to the husband's family, and self-sacrifice is a highly regarded virtue that subjugates the woman at every level of her existence. Kamat (2003) described the unique problems of Indian women as those of the dowry system, the desire for male progeny, unequal shares of inheritance because married girls are not considered part of the

---

[1]Dowry was the ceremonious property, money, and jewelry given to women during wedding as *Stree Dhan* (women's money) to safeguard her rights and be used in times of problems. This also added to her status in her marital home. Over the years, this practice has been extensively exploited, where the demands for marriage have led to grave consequences and women have been exploited, abused, committed suicide, and burned to death for their money. The system continues to exist despite several governmental reforms.

family, and the lack of public toilets, a hygiene problem that keeps most women from getting out of the house.

However, over the years the Indian government's efforts regarding economic liberalization and constitutional amendments to reserve quotas for women in educational institutions and local self-government have had a positive impact, in terms of not only increasing their educational levels but also their political participation. Urban migrations have gradually moved families to the cities, providing women with greater independence and opportunities to participate in social activities. With the increase in the literacy rate, urban women are exploring a diversity of occupations. Women's issues are being treated with much more compassion, which is a welcome sign (Anand, 1992; Calman, 1992; Mohanty, 1991; Sinha,1993).

MEDIA INTERFACE AND THE PORTRAYAL OF WOMEN IN ADVERTISING

The modernization of Indian women is not a reflection of "Westernization," but an evolutionary change that is taking place in Indian society and media. This process of change began in the early 1980s, when the state-owned Indian television *Doordarshan* (literally meaning distance viewing) started beaming afternoon programs for women that included topics on careers, health, homemaking, economic independence, and social and legal issues in addition to entertainment programs. These programs made a difference to the lives of middle-class women and enhanced the lives of their families. Further, women-oriented soap operas showed women playing strong roles and fighting for their rights, clearly inspiring the more submissive and subjugated Indian women (Joshi, 1991; Karan, 1990; Radhakrishna, 2001; Thakur, 1997).

Literature on the representation of Indian women in advertising has been interesting and extensive, yet conflicting. Early literature on women in advertising has reflected the gender biases, "western influences" and negative portrayals of female stereotypes. For the most part women were shown in submissive roles or being exploited for their bodies (Coonrod, 1998; Gail, 1990; Joshi, 1991; Kamat, 2003; Kumar, 1993; Sinha, 1993). The dominant role for women in advertising has historically been identified as that of domestic help or the "showcase" wife or mother. Stereotypically, Indian women in advertising were expected to be coy, submissive, and long suffering, and of course beautiful, so they could be used to sell beauty products (Indian women online, 1999). Das (2000) recorded that, though there has been a change in the status and roles of women in the country, the media have been slow to capture and reflect this trend. She attributed this largely to the business of beauty culture in the modernized world where commercial messages continue to project stereotypical and unequal representations of women.

Over the years, there have been noticeable changes in the representation of women in advertising, particularly since the 1990s (Ahmed, 1998; Griffin, Viswanath & Schwartz, 1994; Joshi, 1991; Radhakrishna 2001). Sengupta and Pashupathi (1996), analyzing the difference between the advertisements of the 1960s and the 1990s, found changes in the portrayal of women, from the traditional to the "modern" women. The woman in the 1960s was either docile or a vamp. Since the 1990s the modern woman is no longer depicted as the sari-clad beauty decked with flowers, thus affirming her secularity. Often she is not portrayed with a shy look (though it is the preferred pose).

Bhagat (2002) found that in the last couple of decades, Indian women have slowly been empowered; socially, educationally and economically. It is only lately that Indian advertising has begun to record this change. In a non-systematic analysis reviewing some of the Indian advertisements on television and magazines, Bonde (2003) exemplifies the changing portrayal of women and men, and attributes it to their changing role in society. He notes that the clothes worn by women in advertisements tell a lot. Today, they are comparable in style and boldness to those worn by women in any other part of the world.

THE MEDIA IN INDIA—THE CONTENT AND CONTEXT OF MAGAZINES FOR WOMEN IN INDIA

India is undergoing a communication revolution and there is an extensive expansion of the media (Singhal & Rogers, 2001). The Indian print industry has been growing at a steady pace despite the threats from the broadcast media and the Internet. There are 52,660 publications of which over 5,364 are dailies, 339 are bi- and tri-weeklies, 17,749 weeklies, 6,553 fortnightlies and 13,616 monthlies. The highest numbers are published in Hindi (the national language), followed by English and other regional languages (Bara, Dasgupta, & Thakur, 2001). There has been a substantial increase in the literacy rate to 65.4%, a record growth of 13% from 1991-2001. In addition, the female literacy rate has also increased to about 55% in the past decade.

Advertising has been the driving force behind the media expansion, and multinational brands entering Indian markets have dominated Indian advertising. Indian advertising agencies, either fully Indian or affiliated with other international agencies (BBDO, O&M, McCann-Ericsson etc.), offer a variety of services, planning local culture-specific campaigns for international brands (Karan & Mathur, 2003).

There has been an increase in the magazines targeted to women in the past decade, both in English and the regional languages. Newspapers also bring out special supplements for women in the magazine sections of the Sunday newspapers. Women's magazines have generally played a significant role as purveyors of values, through their direct engagement with the reader's lives and in shaping women's femininity and identity. At times they have also set the agenda, telling women what to think about and what to do about themselves and other people such as their husbands, extended families and children. Women's magazines also foster a "cult of femininity" (Ferguson, 1983; Goffman, 1976; Shaw, 1999; Shevelow, 1989; Winship, 1991). Lont (1995) described women's magazines as vehicles that shape the ways in which women and men see the ideal woman. Magazines have affected Indian women's lives in many ways, evidenced by magazines such as *Femina, Women's Era, New Woman, Sarita*, and so forth. These magazines for women generally purveyed fashion, cooking, recreation, stories and at most profiled a few women achievers, evident in the two popular English women's magazines, *Eves' Weekly* and *Femina*.

Over the years some crusading women journalists created the required change to help bring Indian women out from their homes and kitchens. Through articles on education, economic independence, politics and political participation, women's rights, rape, dowry, and sexual harassment, these magazines have helped empower women. Though *Eves' Weekly* closed down recently, *Femina* continues to be a leading women's magazine with a tagline *"for the woman of substance."* It has, over the years, sponsored the Ms. India contest and has sent Indian beauties to world pageants, which has directly and indirectly triggered the extensive beauty business in the country. Apart from the English magazines, the regional language magazines, especially in Hindi, Bengali, Malayalam and Tamil, are also extremely popular. *Grihshobha* and *Sarita,* the popular Hindi magazines used for the analysis in this chapter, have high circulations and readership in the northern states of India.

Marketers are constantly using women's magazines to promote a variety of products and services. Therefore, the portrayal of women in advertisements in magazines should reflect their social representation, images, and occupational roles. The images or beauty types of women, the products they advertise, their gaze, the occupational roles they are shown in, all are useful for monitoring the changes in their representation. It is essential to record the change that is taking place in the cultural stereotypes and the ways in which the portrayal of traditional Indian women is changing in print advertisements.

BEAUTY BUSINESS—
A GROWING INDUSTRY

The impact of globalization has introduced a plethora of products that occupy market shelf spaces targeting women with increased purchasing power. Advertising has fully exploited every market opportunity and has kept pace with the changing dynamics in Indian society. It is appropriate to mention here that Indian advertising has itself matured over the years. It had three major boosts: spurts of reforms in the early and middle years of the 1980s; the economic liberalization policies started in the mid-1990s with the launch of Star TV, the Pan-Asian satellite television network based in Hong Kong; and the subsequent launch of several satellite and cable channels in India.

Beauty as a constructed reality is also a source of pleasure and empowerment among women. Women's self-esteem also seems to be related to their own physical well-being and attractiveness (Harter, 1993; Striegel-Moore, Silberstein, & Rodin, 1986). Historical evidence reveals how Indian women have traditionally used herbs, creams made from edible flowers, fruits, and grains to make themselves beautiful and attractive to men. The regular flow of products and the marketing of good looks through fashion shows, beauty contests, careers in modeling, and of course, advertising have created widespread awareness in women about beauty. In fact, girls as young as 8 years old are now becoming beauty and weight conscious. Beauty parlors have mushroomed in the cities and can also be found in towns and villages. These trends have contributed to a greater consciousness of the concept of beauty, vastly complimenting women's changing attitudes towards looking and feeling good.

Another factor that has triggered the beauty business in India is the world's recognition of Indian beauties at international pageants. Since 1993, Indian beauties have won international beauty pageants, becoming Miss World, Miss Universe, and Miss Asia-Pacific as well as Mrs. World. These women have become role models to the young aspirants as well as cosmetic marketers; both international and national brands have cashed in on the beauty trend. Extensive media coverage and advertisements show young and old women how to reach their goals of looking good, and women's magazines are full of ads for a variety of products—particularly beauty products—and clothing.

The proliferation of global brands entering Indian markets has also increased the use of Caucasian models in Indian advertising. Wilk (1996) questions whether people of other cultures really find these western models attractive. A study of the portrayal of women in advertisements in women's magazines in three countries—Singapore, Taiwan, and the United States—

(Frith, Cheng & Shaw, 2004) found that there was a high percentage of Caucasian models used in Asian women's magazines. Thus, the questions addressed in this study will be: What are the races of the models used in Indian print advertising? What are the products being advertised? What occupational roles are Indian women shown in and what beauty types are being used in Indian women's magazines?

METHODOLOGY

In order to examine the ways in which women are portrayed in leading Indian women's magazines, the technique of content analysis was used. Content analysis is an effective tool for mass communication research because it provides data that is reliable, systematic, and objective. Kripendorff (2004) defines it as a research technique for making replicable and valid inferences from texts (or other meaningful matter) to the contexts of their use. Wimmer and Dominick (2003) define content analysis as an efficient way to investigate the content of the media and compare it to real-world situations.

A sample of four leading English and Hindi magazines published monthly in India was selected for the study. These included *Femina*, with a readership of 1.73 million, and *Women's Era*, with a readership of 1.1 million, to represent the English segment of readers. *Sarita*, a Hindi magazine with a readership of 4 million and *Griha Shoba* (Beautiful Home) with a readership of 673,500 (the second highest readership in the country) were chosen to represent the Hindi segment. *Femina*, which for over four decades has advertised itself as a magazine for the *woman of substance* and the *voice of the Indian woman* is popular among the upper- and middle-income groups.[2] *Women's Era* tends to target the English speaking middle-class segments. Similarly in the northern states of the country, where Hindi is the dominant language, *Sarita* and *Griha Shoba* are targeted at the high- and middle-income groups. All four magazines extensively cover women's issues, fashion, home décor and fiction stories along with advertisements of products and services targeting women. Samples of four issues of each magazine from the 12-month period between the years 2002-2003 were selected for the study.

---

[2]The Indian middle class is projected to be around 200-300 million and is constantly increasing as indicated by the standard of living, the purchasing power parity, and the gross domestic product (GDP). The country achieved an average growth rate of 8% in the years 2004-2005, an increase from 6% in the previous years. In 2006, the GDP was US $3,737.00. If growth continues at its recent pace, over 100 million people are expected to move out of poverty over the next two decades. (Source: http://en.wikipedia.org/wiki/Standard_of_living_in_India, http://www.thehindubusinessline.com/2005/01/22/stories/2005012201860700.htm

The unit of analysis was mainly half or full-page advertisements, containing at least one woman displayed in a medium to close-up shot. In the Hindi magazines, half-or quarter-page advertisements that had a woman in them were considered. Advertisements that did not have a woman were not coded. For reviewing the content categories, one English-language and one Hindi magazine were coded independently for all the variables by the author and a colleague and tested for intercoder reliability. The percentage of agreement for the five categories ranged between 88-92%, which is above the minimum expected intercoder reliability (Holsti, 1969; Kassarjian, 1977; Riffe, Lacy, & Drager, 1996). Both coders worked together on other issues of the magazines. A total of 373 advertisements were coded across all the magazines.

Advertisements were classified according to *beauty types, occupational roles, products advertised, race and gaze* (see operational definitions in Appendix A). The five major beauty types included Classic/Elegant, Cute, Sex Kitten, and Trendy. The products advertised were classified after an analysis of schemes followed by Venkatesan and Losco (1975), Frith, Cheng and Shaw (2004), Solomon, Ashmore, and Longo (1992), and Englis, Solomon, and Ashmore (1994), and new categories were added if there was a significant presence of another product category in the country (see Appendix A). Intercoder reliability was established before the final analysis was carried out. The variables were cross-tabulated in order to find out what are the current portrayals of Indian women in magazine advertisements.

ANALYSIS AND DISCUSSION— THE PORTRAYAL OF WOMEN IN INDIAN ADVERTISEMENTS

Among the total advertisements coded, marked differences were observed in the number of advertisements in English and Hindi magazines. Three-fourths of the advertisements were in the English magazines, compared to only a quarter in the Hindi magazines. Within the English magazine segment, almost half the advertisements (47.2%) were in *Femina* and 27.6% in *Women's Era,* while the rest (25.1%) were in the Hindi magazines. Despite the flow of multinational products into Indian markets through extensive advertising, the use of Caucasian models was found to be low. There was a greater tendency to use Indian models in advertisements, as a majority (84%) of models were Indian. Only 16% of models were Caucasian. If the models were Caucasian, they were largely used in advertisements in the English-language magazines.

BEAUTY TYPES—RACE AND ETHNICITY

In the representation of women in Indian magazines, two main beauty types emerged as most popular: Cute (30.2%) and the Classic/Elegant (29.6%). Together they represented almost 60% of all portrayals. The other beauty types used were Sex Kittens (23.7%) and Trendy (14%). Interestingly, the beauty type used most often for Caucasians (62.9%) was Sex Kitten, whereas Indian women were used in this way only about 16% of the time (see Appendix B, Table 6.1).

The Classic/Elegant beauty type was the most common portrayal for Indian women (34%) in the advertisements. The models were elegantly clad in saris or *salwar kameez* (popularly called the Punjabi suit—long tunic worn with loose pants), with well-groomed hair and accessories such as jewelry, footwear, and matching handbags. The Cute beauty types (31.7%) were used for younger, more independent and casual Indian women whose appearance was in contrast to the subdued and traditional Indian woman in the Classic/Elegant beauty type.

Indian women were also shown as Sex Kitten (16%) or Trendy (about 16%). These could be new, emerging stereotypes for young Indian women as they move away from the demure and submissive stereotypes of the past. Certainly, the portrayal of Indian women as the Sex Kitten wearing sexy attire or tight revealing clothes and posed in a seductive way is quite different from the older portrayals of the shy and submissive Indian woman (Ahmed, 1998; Radhakrishan, 2001).

A similar attitude change is reflected in the representation of women as Trendy, in clothes, hair, and general casual appearance. In the Indian context a casual appearance, showing women mostly appearing in western attire or stylistic versions of Indian costumes with a carefree independent look, may be reflective of modernization of the Indian women. Overall, with an almost equal percentage of Indian models distributed in the Classic/Elegant (34%) and Cute (31.7%) categories, we can see that Indian advertisers are being cautious and playing it safe, and also are trying to strike a balance between the modern and the traditional.

PRODUCTS ADVERTISED

In the analysis of products advertised in the Indian magazines, it was found that over two-thirds of advertisements were geared to personal care products; cosmetics, clothes and fashion accessories for the Indian woman, who is more conscious of looking and feeling good. More than a quarter of the advertisements were for beauty and personal care products (27.1%), followed by women's clothing (20.9%) and women's accessories (11.5%) (see Table 6.2).

Other product categories that appeared frequently were medicines and drugs (13.4%) and food products (2.1%), as well as home appliances *(6.7%)*. All of these products were most probably aimed at married women with families for the burden of housework, as well as for the working woman. Medicines and other drugs, an important category, was related mainly to birth control pills that are being extensively advertised to control the Indian population.

The miscellaneous products *(16.9%)* category covered an interesting mix of advertisements that related to service industries such as banks, insurance and financial companies, hotels and airlines, and products such as cell phones, luggage, exercise equipment, and cars, which would previously have been targeted at men. Their inclusion in women's magazines is an indication of the recognition of changing status and the empowerment of women in decision making.

GAZE

Gaze refers to whether the model's eyes look directly into the camera or away from it. Indian women would traditionally shy away from the camera unlike Western women who often look directly into the camera (Frith & Mueller, 2003). The largely favored pose of looking directly *into* the camera is a dynamic projection of women who can hold their own ground, whereas looking *away* from the camera is seen as a nondynamic, submissive/subordinate trait, a traditional projection that continues to be favored, as seen in the literature (Goffman, 1976). In terms of gaze almost two-thirds (62.5%) of Indian women looked directly into the camera (see Table 6.3). Contrary to what was expected, this finding suggests that Indian women are becoming self-confident and assertive. It might also suggest that certain poses and gazes are becoming globalized (Griffin, Viswanath, & Schwartz, 1994).

REPRESENTATION OF WOMEN IN OCCUPATIONAL ROLES AND BEAUTY TYPES

The representations of women in occupational roles help us to see whether there are new modern stereotypes of Indian women being shown in advertising. However, it was found that identification of the occupational roles in print advertisements was often difficult to assess. Over one-fourth of the women in the print advertisements were projected in glamorous or decorative roles (26.8%), followed by housewives (20.1%), entertainment celebrities (14.7%), and recreational roles (7%). The role least represented was professional women (5.9%). Although India has a large number of professionally qualified women, the same trend is not reflected in advertising. Approximately 25% of all the ads were coded as "can't say" because it was hard to determine the occupational role in many ads (see Table 6.4).

The roles become clearer if occupational role projection is correlated with product categories advertised (see Table 6.5). The professional roles (63.6%) projected were appropriate for products and services that included mobile phones, cars, insurance and banking services, hotels, airlines, and home appliances (18.2%). Therefore, the portrayal of women as professionals continues to be low, but given the nature of the products, it is natural. Celebrities from the entertainment world, largely film and television personalities, are used in the beauty and personal care products and women's accessories and clothing. In other categories, celebrities still rank behind housewives in terms of versatility in promotion of a variety of products. In the housewife category, the classification is limited by the operational definition of women engaged in housework and appears in the traditional wife and mother roles in clothes, accessories, or with children. Unlike other occupational role projections, the housewife type has been used to promote every product category, but ranks much lower in promoting beauty and glamour products. The recreational women rank next to the housewife as a versatile type in terms of promoting a wide variety of products. The decorative models are seldom used for promoting cleaning products or food but rather for beauty and personal care products. Race appears to be a significant variable in the occupational roles. The Indian models were most often used as housewives (22.7%), whereas in decorative roles Indian women were shown 29.1% of the time and Caucasians 16.1%. There were near equal role projections in the professional roles (with 6.1% Indian and 4.8% Caucasian) and celebrity (16.1% Caucasian and 14.5% Indian).

CONCLUSION

As the objectives of the study were to monitor the representation of women, it was found that the portrayal of women in Indian advertisements is not just of the decorative and submissive woman, but also, women of various beauty types and occupational roles. The findings debunk some of expected stereotypes of Indian women and are interesting in terms of the use of women as *social* objects in advertisements. Whereas Frith, Cheng and Shaw

(2004) found that Chinese women were seldom used in sexual or suggestive poses, this does not hold true of Indian women in advertising. Thus, Asian cultures differ in the use of women's bodies. Moreover, if gaze was an indication of empowerment, a majority of Indian models looked at the camera, and this suggests that Indian women have moved beyond the shy, submissive, traditional stereotype.

The recognition of the many roles that women play in advertising has left little doubt that changes in the economic and social structures of modern India are reflected in the modernization of the representation of Indian women. Though we cannot evaluate the status of women from representations in the media, nonetheless there is a need to see the shift in representation as a leading light in improving the status and portrayal of women in society. This is widely evident in the profile of women's representation in the media as well as in advertising. In the advertisements analyzed, it is evident that women are gradually moving away from the traditional stereotypical submissive roles of mother and homemaker, to a modern appearance, portrayed through the beauty types such as the Cute and Trendy and also empowered as Classic beauties who could gaze into the camera with self-confidence.

The Indian media of late has recognized the changing status and role of women, which is reflected in the coverage given to and for women. While television has exhibited "women power" in all its forms in the popular women-oriented serials, women's magazines have slowly and steadily contributed to the change in the women themselves and the attitude of the society towards them. Women's magazines have reminded women of their duties and responsibilities by offering a forum for sharing problems, focusing on equality, covering social and economic issues concerning women along with articles on beauty, fashion, and health. These magazines have also contributed to helping women to develop their personalities and increase their self-esteem. Advertising has been depicting women in a variety of roles. Because advertiser's business platforms and objectives are commercial, stereotypical images do continue to be projected along with the modern and empowered women.

This systematic analysis of the role of women in Indian magazine advertising reveals the evolving changes in the representation of women in magazine advertising, debunking many presumed portrayals and projections. In Indian women's magazines, Indian models dominate advertising, but a good number of Caucasian models have entered the Indian scene, bringing with them international brands of beauty products and clothing. It's interesting to note that many multinational companies are also gradually moving towards using Indian models for advertising their products in India.

Analysis of advertising to Indian women shows that the preferred beauty stereotypes are Classic/Elegant and Cute, but the emerging types are

Trendy and Sex Kittens. Whatever might be said about the so-called exploitation of the women's bodies in the West, it does not yet appear to hold true in India. In three product categories the Sex Kitten projection overtakes other forms—dominantly in personal and beauty care, and marginally in women's clothing and other products. Everywhere else, advertisers have used more conventional beauty types.

Similar is the case of representation of occupational roles. Findings in this study reveal that women are being represented in professional roles only when the products or services called for such role representation. Though literature suggested that Indian women might not look directly into the camera, analysis of gaze did not reflect this. The research found that almost two-thirds of Indian women looked directly at the camera.

In conclusion, there is a definite shift in focus in the portrayal of beauty types of women in the women's magazines in India. Modernization is reflected in the portrayal of women in terms of dress, occupation, gaze, and products advertised. The art of looking and feeling good is the new mantra for the representation of beauty. The global processes are fast working in India with the process of modernization; the cultural manifestation of this change is the shift in the beauty types from the shy, submissive family type role to playing a more confident enlightened woman. These new modern stereotypes may be the "beauty types" of the future Indian women.

APPENDIX A

OPERATIONAL DEFINITIONS

Classification of 'Beauty Types'

- Classic/elegant: The woman is slightly older than an average fashion model, feminine, usually wears soft, feminine apparel and is not heavily accessorized.
- Cute: The woman wears casual attire, youthful appearance, and an interesting combination of awkwardness and naturalness, as though the model was caught off-guard. Awkwardness (with small ponytails, wearing clothes more suitable for younger age groups) is a crucial component of cute.
- Sex kitten/sensual: Usually wears sexy attire, lingerie, and revealing or tight clothes. Often does not look directly into camera.
- Trendy: Wears faddish clothes and displays oversized accessories, colorful attire, and often wild or tousled hair.
- Others: Other beauty types that do not fall into the above categories.

Product Categories

The product categories were classified as: beauty and personal care, women's clothing, women's accessories, cleaning products, food and food products, medicines and drugs and miscellaneous. In the Indian magazines, several time- and energy-saving home appliances like washing machines, microwave ovens, cooking ranges, and so on, were advertised in the Indian magazines but not in the others, and hence this category was also added.

Ethnicity: The ethnicity of the models was coded to find whether the models were Indian or Caucasian. The Indian models could be from any part of the country and Caucasian models are ethnically white in appearance and usually American or European.

Gaze was defined as the look in the eyes of the woman in the advertisement. Gaze of the models was coded to find the level of empowerment. It was classified as the model looking directly into the camera or looking away from it. This was done to measure the extent to which the models had the shy submissive look or expressed power in terms of looking directly at the camera. The differences in the gaze between the Indian and the Caucasian models were analyzed. Therefore, advertisements not showing women's eyes or with the model wearing sunglasses were excluded from the sample.

Occupational Roles

Professional. Women projected in a career or business. Images that showed them in some occupations in terms of dress or using accessories typical of the profession were used for coding.

Celebrities. These included the people from the entertainment world and those famous for other recreations or sports. These included popular film and television stars, sports personalities, models, and so on.

Housewife. Women represented as housewives in family roles, as mothers with children or carrying out household activities, dressed in traditional styles.

Recreational. The model is dressed in a way that suggests she is engaged in some recreational activity such as visiting friends, shopping, sports and other outdoor activities, walking or jogging.

Decorative roles. The model is not depicted as having a functional role, such as mother, worker, shopper or movie star. She is shown only for her attractiveness and beauty.

Can't say/others. This category covered any other roles that did not fit in the above categories and when it was difficult to ascertain the occupational role of the model.

APPENDIX B

Table 6.1
Portrayal of Beauty Types and Ethnicity of Models
in Indian Magazine Advertisements

BEAUTY TYPE	ETHNICITY					
	Caucasian		Indian		Total	
	Freq.	%	Freq.	%	Freq.	%
Classic/elegant	5	8.1	105	34.0	110	29.6
Cute	14	22.6	98	31.7	112	30.2
Sex Kitten/Sensual	39	62.9	49	15.9	88	23.7
Trendy	3	4.8	49	15.9	52	14.0
Others	1	1.6	8	2.6	9	2.4

Table 6.2
Product Categories Advertised in Indian Magazines

PRODUCT CATEGORIES	FREQ.	%
Beauty and personal care	101	27.1
Women's clothing	78	20.9
Women's accessories	43	11.5
Cleaning products	5	1.3
Food and food products	8	2.1
Medicines and drugs	50	13.4
Home appliances	25	6.7
Miscellaneous	63	16.9
Total	373	100.0

Table 6.3
Gaze and Race of Models

GAZE	RACE					
	Caucasian		Indian		Total	
	Freq.	%	Freq.	%	Freq.	%
Looks directly into camera	34	54.8	193	62.5	227	61.2
Looks away from camera	28	45.2	116	37.5	144	38.8
Total	62	100.0	209	100.0	361	100.0

Table 6.4
Occupational Role of the Models

ROLE	FREQ.	%
Professional	22	5.9
Entertainer/celebrity	55	14.7
Family oriented/homemaker	75	20.1
Recreational/sportswoman	26	7.0
Decorative/pretty woman	100	26.8
Can't say	95	25.5
Total	373	100.0

Table 6.5
Product Categories Advertised and Occupational Role of Models

PRODUCT CATEGORY	OCCUPATIONAL ROLE OF MODEL						
	Professional	Celebrity	Homemaker	Recreational	Decorative	Others	Total
Beauty, personal care	4.5% (1)	30.9% (17)	13.3% (10)	19.2% (5)	37.0% (37)	32.6 % (31)	27.1% (101)
Woman's clothing	(0)	21.8% (12)	16.0% (12)	23.1% (6)	30.0% (30)	18.9% (18)	20.9% (78)
Women's accessories	(0)	23.6% (13)	1.3% (1)	7.7% (2)	19.0% (19)	8.4% (8)	11.5% (43)
Cleaning products	(0)	(0)	5.3% (4)	3.8% (1)	(0)	(0)	1.3% (5)
Food, food products	(0)	1.8% (1)	9.3% (7)	(0)	(0)	(0)	2.1% (8)
Medicines, drugs	13.6% (3)	1.8% (1)	20.0% (15)	15.4% (4)	4.0% (4)	24.2% (23)	13.4% (50)
Home appliances	18.2% (4)	3.6% (2)	14.7% (11)	3.8% (1)	3.0% (3)	4.2% (4)	6.7% (25)
Miscellaneous	63.6% (14)	16.4% (9)	20.0% (15)	26.9% (7)	7.0% (7)	11.6% (11)	16.9.%(63)

Table 6.6. Ethnicity and Occupational Role of the Models

ETHNICITY	OCCUPATIONAL ROLE						
	Professional	Celebrity	Housewife	Recreational	Decorative	Others	Total
Caucasian	4.8% (3)	16.1% (10)	4.8% (3)	1.6% (1)	16.1% (10)	56.5% (35)	100% (62)
Indian	6.1% (19)	14.6% (45)	22.7% (70)	8.1% (25)	29.1% (90)	19.4% (60)	100% (309)

REFERENCES

Ahmed, N. (1998, Spring). Mass media stereotyping in the 1990s: A cross-cultural perspective. *Journal of Information Ethics*, 68–78.

Anand, A. (1992). *The power to change: Women in the third world redefine their environment* (pp. 1-21). New Delhi: Kali for Women.

Bara, J., Dasgupta, D.P., & Thakur, S.S. (2001). *Mass media 2001.* New Delhi: Publications Division, Ministry of Information and Broadcasting, Government of India.

Bhagat, R. (2002). Can new image hide old scars? *The Hindu Business Line* (Internet Edition) (http://blonnet.com/2002/08/23/stories).

Bhatt, B. (1991). *Portrayal of women in prime time television programmes.* Unpublished M. Phil. Dissertation, Department of Home Science, Extension and Communication, The MS University of Baroda, India.

Bonde, P. (2003). *The bold and the beautiful* (http://www.geocites.com/madison Avenue/Boardroom/3533/page2.1.html).

Butler, J. (1990). *Gender trouble: Feminism and the subversion of identity.* New York: Routledge.

Calman, L. (1992). *Towards empowerment: Women and movement politics in India.* Boulder, CO: Westview Press.

Caplan, L. (1984). Bridegroom price in urban India: Class, caste and dowry evil among Christians in Madras. *Man, 19*(2), 216-233.

Census of India (2001). Government of India. http://www.censusindia.net/results/resultsmain.html

Chang, W.H., Palasthira, T.S., & Kim, K.K. (1995). *Rise of Asian advertising.* Seoul, Korea: NANAM International House.

Choudhary, M. (1992). Towards a positive portrayal of women in the media. A review of the literature. 1980-1990. Delhi: WFS Women's Feature Service

Coonrod, C.S. (1998). *Chronic hunger and the status of women in India* (http://www.thp.org/reports/indiawom.htm).

Das, M. (2000, November). Men and women in Indian magazine advertisements: A preliminary report. *Sex Roles: A Journal of Research, 43*(9), 699–718.

Desai, N., & Patel, V. (1985). *Indian women: Change and challenge in the international decade (1975–1985).* New Delhi: Popular Prakashan.

Dreze, J., & Sen, A. (1996). *India: Economic development and social opportunity.* New Delhi: Oxford University Press.

Edwards, L., & Roces, M. (Eds). (2000). *Women in Asia: Tradition, modernity and globalization.* St. Leonard, NSW: Allen & Unwin.

Englis, B., Solomon, M., & Ashmore, R. (1994). Beauty before the eyes of beholders: The cultural encoding of beauty types in magazine advertising and music television. *Journal of Advertising, 23*(2), 49-63.

Ewen, S., & Ewen, E. (1982). *Channels of desire: Mass images and the shaping of American consciousness.* New York: McGraw-Hill.

Ferguson, J.H., Kreshel, P.J., & Tinkham, S.F. (1990). In the pages of Ms.: Sex role portrayals of women in advertising. *Journal of Advertising, 19*(1), 40-41.

Ferguson, M. (1983). *Forever feminism: Women's magazines and the cult of feminity.* London: Heinemann.

Frith, K.T., Cheng.H., & Shaw P. (2004). Race and beauty: A comparison of Asian and Western models in women's magazines advertisements. *Sex Roles, 50*, 53-61.

Frith, K.T., & Mueller, B. (2003). *Advertising and societies: Global issues.* New York: Peter Lang.

Gail, O. (1990). *Violence against women. New movements and new theories in India.* New Delhi: Kali for Women.

Gallagher, M. (1981). *Unequal opportunities: The case of women and the media.* Paris: UNESCO.

Ganguly-Scrase, R. (2000). Diversity and the status of women: The Indian experience. In L. Edwards & R.M. Roces (Eds.), *Women in Asia: Tradition, modernity and globalization* (pp. 85-111). St. Leonard, NSW: Allen & Unwin.

Geraghty, C. (2000). Representation and popular culture: Semiotics and the construction of meaning. In J. Curran & M. Gurevitch (Eds.), *Mass media and society* (3rd ed., pp. 362-375). London: Oxford University Press.

Goffman, E. (1976). *Gender advertisements.* New York: Harper-Collins.

Government of India. (2002). *India year book—2002.* New Delhi: Ministry of Information and Broadcasting.

Griffin, M., Viswanath, K., & Schwartz, D. (1994). Gender advertising in the US and India: Exporting cultural stereotypes. *Media, Culture & Society, 16*, 486-507.

Harter, S. (1993). Causes and consequences of low self-esteem in children and adolescents. In R. F. Baumeister (Ed.), *Self-esteem: The puzzle of low self-regard* (pp. 87-116). New York: Plenum Press.

Hawley, J.S., & Wulff, D.M. (1996). *Devi: Goddesses of India.* Berkeley: University of California Press.

Holsti, O. (1969). *Content analysis for the social sciences and humanities.* Reading: Addison-Wesley.

Indian Women Online (1999). *Portrayal of women in advertising.* Retrieved from Viewers Forum, Lucknow Chapter, http://www.viewersforum.com/vf/lucknow.htm.

Joshi, I. (1991). *Women dimension on television: Policy, personnel and programme.* New Delhi. Concept.

Kalia, N.N. (1988). Images of men and women in Indian textbooks. *Comparative Education Review, 24*, 209–223.

Kamat, J. (2003). *Gandhi and status of women.* http://www.kamat.com/mmgandhi/gwomen. htm.

Kassarjian, H.H. (1977). Content analysis in consumer research. *Journal of Marketing Research, 4*, 8-18.

Karan, K. (1990). *Sociological impact of television programmes on women of Hyderabad and Secunderabad.* Unpublished M.Phil Thesis, Department of Sociology, Osmania University, Hyderabad, India.

Karan, K., & Mathur, R.R. (2003). India. In A. Goonasekhara, C.H. Lee, & S. Venkatraman (Eds.), *Asian communication handbook 2003* (pp. 93-122). Singapore: Asian Media Information and Communication Center and Nanyang Technological University.

Krippendorf K. (2004). *Content analysis: An introduction to its methodology* (2nd ed.). Thousand Oaks, CA: Sage.

Krishnan, P., & Dighe, A. (1990). *Affirmation and denial: Construction of feminity on Indian television.* Newbury Park, CA: Sage.

Kumar, R. (1993). *The history of doing: An illustrated account of women's rights and feminism in India.* London: Verso.

Lont, C.M. (1995). *Women and media: Content, careers and criticism.* Belmont, CA: Wadsworth.

Mani, L. (1990). Contentious traditions: The debate on sati in colonial India. In K. Sangari & S. Wai (Eds.), *Recasting women: Essays in Indian colonial history* (pp. 88-126). New Brunswick, NJ: Rutgers University Press.

Mehta, M. (1997). *Marketing women's health through television.* Ahmedabad: Indian Space Research Organization.

Miller, B. (1981). *The endangered sex: Neglect of the female children in rural North India.* Ithaca: Cornell University Press.

Mills, B. (1995). Attack of the widow ghosts: Gender, death, and modernity in northeast Thailand. In A. Ong & M. G. Peletz (Eds.), *Bewitching women, pious men: Gender and body politics in Southeast Asia* (pp. 244-273). Berkeley and Los Angeles: University of California Press.

Mohanty, C.T. (1991). Under western eyes: Feminist scholarship and colonial discourses. In C.T. Mohanty, A. Russo, & L. Torres (Eds.), *Third world women and the politics of feminism* (pp. 51-80). Bloomington: Indiana University Press.

Munshi, S. (2001). *Images of Indian women in the media.* http://www.iias.nl/iiasn/iiasn5/munshi.html.

Prasad, K. (2005). *Women and media: Challenging feminist discourse.* New Delhi: The Women Press.

Radhakrishna C. (2001). *The image of women in Indian television.* Women in Action, http://www.isiswomen.org/pub/wia/wia101/media.html.

Rege, S. (1995). Caste and gender: The violence against women in India. In P. G. Jogdand (Ed.), *Dalit women in India: Issues and perspectives.* New Delhi: Gyan.

Rifffe, D., Lacy, S., & Drager, M.W. (1996). Sample size in content analysis of weekly news magazines. *Journalism and Mass Communication Quarterly, 73*(3), 635-644.

Sangari, K., & Vaid, S. (1994). *Women and culture.* Mumbai, Research Centre for Women's Studies. SNDT Women's University.

Sengupta, S., & Pashupathi, K. (1996). Advertising in India: The winds of change. In K.T. Frith (Ed.), *Advertising in Asia: Communication, culture and consumption.* Ames: Iowa University Press.

Shaw, P. (1999). Internalization of the women's magazine industry in Taiwan: Context, process and influence. *Asian Journal of Communication, 9*(2), 17-28.

Sharma, U. (1985). Dowry in India: Its consequences for women. In R. Hirchchon (Ed.), *Women as property.* London: Croom Helm.

Shevelow, K. (1989). *Women and print culture: Construction of femininity in the early periodicals.* London: Routledge.

Singhal, A., & Rogers, E. (2001). *India's communication revolution: From bullock carts to cyber marts.* New Delhi: Sage.

Sinha, A.M. (1993). *Women in a changing society.* New Delhi: Ashish.

Solomon, M.R., Ashmore, R., & Longo, L.C. (1992). The beauty match up hypothesis: Congruence between types of beauty and product images in advertising. *Journal of Advertising 21,* 23-24.

Striegel-Moore, R. H., Silberstein, L.R., & Rodin, J. (1986). Toward an understanding of risk factors for bulimia. *American Psychologist, 42,* 247-263.

Thakur, B.S. (1997). *Media utilization for the development of women and children.* New Delhi: Concept.

Venkatesan, M., & Losco, J. (1975). Women in magazine ads: 1959-1971. *Journal of Advertising Research, 15,* 49-54.

Wilk, R. (1996). Beauty industries in East Asia. http://72.14.235.104/ search?q=cache:uX1aFFb1oiEJ:www.aasianst.org/absts/1999abst/inter/i-190. htm+Richard+Wilk+on+caucasian+models&hl=en&ct=clnk&cd=3.

Wimmer, R., & Dominick, J. (2003). *An introduction to mass media research* (7th ed.). Singapore: Wadsworth.

Winship, J. (1991). *Inside women's magazines.* London: Pandora.

7

Beauty and the Beast

Economic Liberalization, Advertising, and the Construction of Beauty in Indian Advertising

Katya Balasubramanian

K. Viswanath

This chapter falls at the intersection of two major debates in media studies—transnational communications and gender advertising—topics that have garnered much attention among scholars and activists. Simultaneously, it draws attention to the role of the glamour-communication industry complex in the export of cultural formats in the specific context of gender advertising (Viswanath & Zheng, 2000). Lastly, as other studies of globalization in different contexts have argued, our chapter demonstrates how contextual and structural forces inform the framing of discourse and the social construction of reality (Fiss & Hirsch, 2005).

We begin this chapter with the premise that the mass media are agents of social control, a function they serve by reflecting, refracting, and amplifying values, opinions, and perceptions of major power groupings in a social system (Tichenor, Donohue, & Olien, 1980; Viswanath & Demers, 1999). The influence of media content on people's perceptions of reality and subsequent actions has been widely documented and debated in media studies literature (Bryant & Zillman, 2002). Although there is a debate over the degree of the influence of media, it is fairly well accepted that media content of different types and genres—entertainment, news, and advertising—does influence different audiences, albeit to different degrees. Among the genres that have been a target of profound interest is advertising, whose influence locally and globally has received considerable attention in media studies (Hovland & Wilcox, 1989; Jamieson & Campbell, 1992; Leiss, Kline, & Jhally, 1986; Schudson, 1984).

More germane, the role of transnational advertising (TNA) has been a topic of intense focus and attention (Lee, 1982; Viswanath & Zheng, 2000). Specifically, a subject of intense speculation and inconsistent evidence is the influence it is purported to have on local cultures and sovereignty, subjects that are both sweeping and less amenable to rigorous empirical inquiry. Yet it is reasonable to assume that the flow of messages and cultural products could have a profound impact on both individuals and institutions. Therefore, there is value in documenting the impact and providing empirical evidence for debates around transnational advertising. This chapter provides limited but specific empirical evidence on the impact of transnational advertising and globalization on local cultural formats in gender advertising, a specificity that allows one to begin to test empirically several assumptions about TNA. We use the liberalization and globalization of the Indian economy as an exemplar to explain how TNA can potentially influence local advertising formats. Specifically, we draw from our program of research on gender advertising to delineate the influence of transnational advertising.

Why Gender Advertising?

Gender displays in advertising are particularly interesting for various reasons. Women in advertising, as several scholars have observed, are posed in conventionalized forms and patterns that repeatedly frame them in relation to other objects or men in consistent and sustained poses (Goffman, 1987; Griffin, Viswanath, & Schwartz, 1994). Moreover, these visual conventions and formats appear to have successfully penetrated across national cultures, a consistency that offers an opportunity for empirical scrutiny of the penetration. By focusing attention on visual conventions and formats associated with advertising images of women, one can "examine both cultural permutations and adaptations of representation and the transfer and diffusion of media practices and media rhetoric transnationally" (Griffin et al., 1994).

Second, advertisements are created to increase consumer demand and communicate meanings, and thus are very carefully planned and produced. The planning and production takes place in an institutional context facilitating transfer of those conventions across different institutions and countries. It is thus amenable to systematic empirical inquiry. Last, the repetitive portrayal of women in advertisements, particularly body images, has been associated with often-undesirable effects such as stereotyping, dissatisfactions with one's body, and even, in some cases, eating disorders. While the behavioral outcomes have been causes of concern, the impact on the intended and unintended audiences' sense of reality and the possible effects of that perceived reality could have profound social and psychological consequences, providing another reason for studying gender advertising.

The Global and Political-Economic Context of Gender Advertising

Over the last 30 years, the debate on transnational advertising (TNA) in the field of international communication focused on the possible effects it is supposed to have on people's values, lifestyles, and attitudes threatening the cultural sovereignty of nation-states (Lee, 1982). This debate, conducted mostly in the foreground of the new world information and communication order (NWICO), has since become muted for a number of reasons. Globalization and interpenetration of global economies have accelerated thanks to multilateral trade agreements, such as the World Trade Organization (WTO), sidelining any objections raised by NWICO proponents. With the fall of the Soviet empire, proponents of the new order lost a major supporter that saw ideological advantages in championing the Third World cause. Lastly, the debate was not helped by the lack of systematic empirical evidence on the impact of foreign media products and practices on the so-called Third World audiences and media. Although the debate has become muted, given the current pace of globalization, studying transnational advertising has never been more relevant or urgent.

The global flow of capital and goods, concomitant with the global flow of cultural goods including television, news, movies, and advertising, has generated attention among activists, media scholars and policymakers over its impact on all aspects of a nation-state: its peoples, institutions, economy, and culture. Any discussion of international advertising therefore cannot be conducted without considering the changes occurring in the larger economic and political arenas. The fundamental premise informing the research reported here is that increasing globalization and the penetration of transnational communication corporations (TCCs) into developing countries influences not only the lifestyles, values, and attitudes of population subgroups, but is also equally likely to influence the professionalism of media practitioners. This transfer of professionalism, along with the mechanisms by which it comes about, has been elegantly described by Golding (1977), who argued that media professionalism is an ideology that has been transferred to the developing countries from the West in parallel to the transfer of technology. It is argued that such a transfer helped achieve an integration of Third World media practitioners into the "dominant global culture of media practices and objectives" that evolved in the industrialized nations by ways of institutional transfer—the opening of offices worldwide, education and training of media professionals modeled on the West, as well as informal socialization.

ADVERTISING, WOMEN, AND THE CONSTRUCTION OF BEAUTY

Like other agents of social control, the news, entertainment, and advertising media have become forces that establish societal norms for what is acceptable and unacceptable, at times even refracting or distorting existing social ideals and norms (Gerbner et al., 2002; Viswanath & Demers, 1999). In their work, Gerbner et. al (2002) suggest that people's ideas of reality are often distorted by media images of that reality, and that this plays an important part in bringing people's ideas in consonance with those reflected in the media. On a similar plane, Bandura (2002) looks at the process by which symbolic communication influences human thought, affect, and action within a social cognitive framework. He emphasizes vicarious learning, learning by observing rather than doing. Bandura claims that any learning done directly, by doing it oneself, can be learned just as well vicariously. Performance or observationally learned behavior depends on the nature of the outcome. People are more likely to model behavior that is associated with positively valued rather than punitive outcomes.

Such modeling of behavior can be directly observed in the fashion and taste industries, which as we will see in the following paragraphs depend heavily on the social prompting power of advertising. By associating models with positively regarded activities, advertisements draw a connection between the observed behavior and the rewards received. This in turn is likely to promote emulation. This suggests that advertising "influences and serves diverse functions—as tutors, social prompters, shapers of values and [conceivers] of reality."

Gender Advertising Effects

Gender advertising has been implicated in imposing pressure on its target audiences—particularly women, though not exclusively so—owing to the standards of beauty set by the media. Ample empirical evidence documents the relationship between gender advertising and body images of women. Myers and Biocca (1992) comment, "Each of the body image messages is just one strike on a chisel sculpting the ideal body image inside a young woman's mind." A woman's perception of her body then is a psychological as well as a sociological construction, influenced to a large extent by social cues obtained from advertising and other programming.

Studies have analyzed the body image portrayal of women in magazines and on television in the United States (Anderson & DiDomenico, 1992; Cusumano & Thompson, 1997; Silverstein, Perdue, Peterson, & Kelly, 1986; Wiseman, Gray, Mosimann, & Ahrens, 1992). The trend in every one of these studies has been toward a thinner, more "tubular" body ideal, showing emphasis on the body size for women much more so than for men. Following the depiction of women in popular American fashion magazines from 1959–1999, Sypeck, Gray, and Ahrens (2004) found not only a decreasing body size of the fashion models but also a dramatic increase in the depiction of the entire bodies of the models, once again only reinforcing the increasing emphasis and value placed on a thinner body size.

Such a trend clearly takes on a much greater meaning when viewed in the context of the role played by the media in society today, as has been discussed earlier. It is this link between media images and their audiences that scholars such as Turner, Hamilton and Jacobs (1997) have sought to better understand. In their study, women subjects were randomly assigned to two groups—one group was exposed to fashion magazines while the control group was exposed to news magazines. They found that those who had been exposed to the fashion images reported a lower satisfaction with their own body image than those who were in the control group, giving the readers a peek into the power of advertising—which creates the "ideal" and then also becomes the benchmark that audiences compare themselves with. Another study by Field et al. (1999) carried out with young school girls from grades 5–12, revealed similar results as the Turner et al. study. On being exposed to fashion magazines, close to half of the girls reported wanting to lose weight. A linear association was found between the frequency of reading women's magazines and the prevalence of having dieted in order to lose weight among these girls. It is hence conceivable that advertising is "priming" or setting the terms for subsequent evaluations of body images, and leading to dissatisfaction (Iyengar & Kinder, 1987).

The pressure to stay thin manifests itself in several ways, from diet consciousness among preteen girls to eating disorders among others. Studies (Zucker et al., 2001) have also found women more likely to smoke or continue smoking as one way of conforming to the body ideal reflected by the media.

GENDER ADVERTISING AND THE EXPORT
OF STEREOTYPES: THE INDIAN EXEMPLAR

Research carried out in this field so far has been largely in the western hemisphere. This is surprising, especially in light of developments in the spread of Western media systems to the developing nations. We make our arguments with a case study from India. If the contention is that media and the advertising agencies impose exogenous ways and foreign values on developing countries' audiences by displaying or broadcasting images based on cultures alien to the local people, then those influences should be more apparent and forceful when the flow is freer. Economic liberalization, as experienced by India during the 1990s, allows for freer international trade and may offer a profound demonstration of the transnational influence.

It is valuable to examine the impact, if any, of transnational advertising on local cultural formats, ideologies, and perceptions, given the full force of globalization that accompanies economic liberalization. Empirical evidence for what happens to local media institutions as a result of liberalization, particularly in advertising, continues to be thin. The lack of empirical evidence is even more palpable in developing economies.

It is against this backdrop that we discuss the impact of economic liberalization and globalization on local advertising formats and content in India. With the liberalization of the Indian economy and the subsequent inflow of transnational corporations, understanding the impact of these economic phenomena on the media and India's culture has become even more relevant. The discussions in this chapter specifically addresses how the larger economic developments in India have influenced the construction of beauty ideals in the media—ideals that have to be either emulated or rejected— immediately before and after liberalization, in 1985 and 1990.

The Liberalization of the Indian Economy
and Media

In 1991, soon after the liberalization of the Indian economy, foreign-owned companies were allowed to enter the country without giving up majority stock ownership. With the prospect of a potentially large consumer base, this act of the government provided the impetus for many companies to enter Indian markets. Table 7.1 (see Appendix) documents the steady increase in the number of foreign companies entering India over time and demonstrates the integration of the Indian economy with the rest of the world.

In addition, several international cable and satellite channels made their debut with the liberalization of the Indian economy. Prior to economic liberalization, the Indian electronic media were strictly controlled by the state, and there were no private television channels. The 1990s witnessed a profound transformation. The entry of foreign media companies offering private cable and satellite television services to Indian audiences led to a proliferation of channels as well as to the diversion of audiences away from the state-owned media towards private TV channels (Viswanath & Karan, 2000). Accordingly, the audiences for these private channels have increased, (Appendix, Table 7.2). For example, according to the Indian National Readership Survey, in 1997 towards the end of our study period, close to a third (31%) of Indian households had cable and satellite television connections and over two-thirds (70%) had television. The numbers have only gone up with close to half of Indian households having cable and satellite television connections according to the most recent readership surveys in 2003. The Indian economy was clearly more closely linked to the world in 1997 than it had been a decade earlier, when television was entirely controlled by the state.

DATA COLLECTION AND SOURCES

Given the changes associated with globalization and liberalization, one might have anticipated some changes in the gender images portrayed in the media over time. We began our examination of the influence of economic liberalization on gender advertising in India by examining changes in portrayals in the media through systematic content analysis. We used focus groups and surveys to study the likely effects on the audience. In this chapter, we draw from our content analysis and focus group data to illustrate the impact of global flows on local media formats with a focus on gender advertising.

Analysis of Gender Advertising

To examine the visual messages communicated by the advertisements, we systematically analyzed ads that portrayed women in three Indian magazines. Content analysis, as Holsti defined it "is any technique for making inferences by objectively and systematically identifying specified characteristics of messages" (1964).

We adapted the coding scheme used by Griffin, Viswanath, and Schwartz (1994) in their visual analyses of gender portrayals in Indian and American magazines that had later expanded to include categories developed by scholars studying body images in the media. Our final coding scheme accounted for (a) the model's skin tone, (b) her figure, (c) her perceived body size, and (d) the cultural indicators or cues that might locate the model in a given cultural context or country.[1]

Media Selection

For the study, we used three popular English-language Indian magazines to examine the evolving concept of beauty reflected in gender advertising. The three magazines chosen for this study were *Femina*, *Cine Blitz*, and *India Today*.

Femina, one of India's premier women's magazines, claims to be the magazine for "the woman of substance." A significant part of the magazine is devoted to issues such as popular clothes designers, acceptable ways of dressing, applying make-up, and so on. The publishers of *Femina* are the organizers of the annual Miss India beauty pageant that has gained tremendous popularity over the past few years—particularly once some of the winners went on to win international pageants.

Cine Blitz, an Indian movie magazine, has a circulation of 216,105 (Ulrich, 1999). The Indian film industry is highly popular and it is the source of many fashions and trends. Both *Cine Blitz* and *Femina* are highly engaging visually, filled with photographs and colorful advertising.

With a circulation of 414,293, *India Today* is India's leading newsmagazine, addressing a gamut of issues facing the country. Although quite different from the other magazines in terms of editorial content, *India Today* nevertheless shares with them an abundance of advertising space.

---

[1]The coding scheme for the analysis, although based on the scheme adopted by Griffin, Viswanath, and Schwartz, was further refined by the coders according to the focus group discussions held in India as part of the study. The final coding scheme used was operationalized on the basis of how women across age groups defined each of these facets of the woman's body size, as well as the terms and words they chose to describe these facets. This coding scheme was found to have a reproducibility of 83.1% across coders and thus settled upon as the final coding scheme to be used. The model's skin tone was divided into five categories—pale/anemic, white, light-skinned, average/light brown, and dark skinned. Similarly, body size was measured as thin, "normal," full figured, obese/overweight, and lastly "can't tell." The model's figure referred more specifically to the model's muscle tone as opposed to the overall body as measured by body size and was defined as twiggy, muscular, "normal," voluptuous, and "can't tell." Finally, cultural indicators providing a cultural context used were those that provided a context of the Indian culture within the advertising such as Indian clothing, and specific cues such as the *bindi* or red dot worn by many Indian women and the *mangalsutra* or necklace worn by married Hindu women. A total of 616 ads were evaluated for the study (250 ads from 1987 and 366 from 1997).

We chose these particular three magazines so we could study advertising in magazines catering to different audiences, thereby minimizing audience-specific biases. We also chose magazines from different publishers to avoid any influence publishers might have on the nature of the advertising across our magazine sample.

Several editions of *India Today* and *Cine Blitz* are available in the market—international as well as Indian. But, considering that the focus of our study was on gender advertising in India, we studied only the Indian editions of these magazines.

Our sample included all advertisements with women models in every issue of the magazines for the years 1987 and 1997. As we averred earlier, the liberalization process began in 1991; thus, selecting these two years' magazine issues allowed us to examine portrayals before and after the start of the liberalization process. Although realizing that a six-year period since liberalization began may not be adequate to fully assess the impact of changing advertising portrayals, we feel that it was sufficient to ascertain some trends.

To examine the impact on audiences, focus groups were conducted during the summer of 1998 with college-going and middle-aged women, both English-speaking and native language speakers. In all, three focus groups were conducted—two with college women, in which one group was comprised mainly of English-speaking students and the other was comprised of students more comfortable in the regional language—Telugu. The third group was conducted with homemakers. All three groups consisted of 7–8 women each and were conducted in Hyderabad, one of India's largest cities. Hyderabad has recently been experiencing a great growth spurt, with several transnational corporations setting up operations there. The rationale behind segmenting the groups as such was to gain a sense of the impact of the media imagery on a cross-section of women. The premise was that although younger women may be more vulnerable to media imagery pertaining to beauty and body size, this vulnerability would also be tempered by the respondent's personal background. Language of comfort is a proxy for the degree of Westernization that the respondents are already accustomed to as well as the nature of media they are more likely to be exposed to. Although focus groups may not provide systematic data, they do give an idea of the potential impact of media images.

"Beauty" Defined

The question that guided our research was whether transnational companies and foreign media outlets bring along with them a new style of advertising and a new genre of images that in turn influence national cultural forms. Our research questions were borne out of certain assumptions that we made prior to the current study. These assumptions were drawn from the broader context of fading cultural boundaries. Our first assumption was that the entrance of the foreign media has idealized a thin body size for women. This was based on a review of literature on the portrayals of women in magazine advertisements in Western media that clearly showed that the media communicate the idea that thin is good and thinner is better (Simmonds, Urbano, Oglivy, & Viswanath, 1997). Although most of the literature was derived from studies of Western media, the assumption is reasonable when one considers the penetration of foreign media outlets in India post-1991. In all our analyses we show the data at two points in time with appropriate statistical tests for significance in change. All advertisements in the magazines that included women's images were selected for analysis. Thus, while the differences in frequency are real differences, we conducted the tests of significance to allow us to argue for generalization to other magazines and media.

Content analysis of the advertisements found that the percentage of models that were coded as "thin" jumped almost ten-fold from 1987 to 1997, and "full figured" women dropped by almost half (see Appendix, Table 7.3). This frequency of portrayals in 1997 is closer to data reported in other studies of magazine advertisements with women in the West (Viswanath & Balasubramanian, 2000).

In addition, as discussed, we coded the model's figures as "muscular," "voluptuous," "twiggy," "normal," or "can't tell." Our data show a two-fold rise in the number of models considered muscular in 1997 from 1987 (Appendix, Table 7.4). On the other hand, ads with women with "voluptuous" figures dropped by more than half. This drop in numbers is particularly interesting, especially as Indian film actresses from past years—many of whom were emulated for their appearance—commonly had so-called "voluptuous" figures. The number of models who were coded as "twiggy" went up most dramatically from 2.6% in 1987 to close to 7 times that at 14.9% in 1997. Further, the assumption that the increasing globalization of media could lead to a blurring of cultural distinctions between the local and global portrayals was tested by looking for evidence of significant changes. We assumed that the increasing penetration of global fashion trends through advertising was likely to result in greater similarities in the portrayals of Indian and Western models and result in the depiction of fewer traditional Indian cultural cues by the models. That is, by depicting these cues the models should be clearly identified as portraying people from India. A total of six cultural cues were identified—glass bangles, a *bindi*, or the red dot worn by Indian women on their forehead, traditional Indian clothing such as a *sari*—six yards of flowing fabric draped around the body—a *mangalsutra* or necklace, and toe rings.

These cultural identifiers, with the exception of the *bindi* and sari, are signs of marriage among Hindu women in India. The *bindi* is worn by women of all ages except for widows. The Sari, traditionally worn by women post adolescence, is now being replaced by the *salwar-kameez*—a pair of loose pants worn with a tunic—among certain groups of Indian women. Across all cultural indicators, we compared the frequency of their use in 1987 with 1997 (see Appendix, Table 7.5).

The frequency of models wearing glass bangles, an important cultural cue, dropped by half between 1987 and 1997 and the difference was statistically significant. Similarly, there were four times as many models wearing a *bindi* in 1987 as there were in 1997. The number of models in Indian clothing fell by a third in the ten-year span and the frequency of models seen wearing a *mangalsutra*, a necklace worn by married Indian women, was, in 1997 ads, exactly half that of 1987. The last variable in our index of cultural cues examined whether the model was wearing toe rings or not. This was the one case where there was no change in the numbers; in both the years, none of the models was seen wearing toe rings.

Another way of "blending in" or fitting in with the rest of the globalizing world would be by highlighting certain physical features over others. One such feature we studied was the skin tone of the models. There was found to be a three-fold increase in the frequency of models with paler skin (see footnote 1). Similarly, there was a doubling in the frequency of lighter-skinned models from 1987 to 1997. Light skin, which has always been considered desirable in Indian society, saw an increased representation between 1987 and 1997, and brown skin was less represented in 1997 than in 1987. The most dramatic decline in representation of skin color was in that of dark skin, which dropped from 9.8% in 1987 to almost one-tenth of that at 1.4% in 1997 (see Appendix, Table 7.6).

The third assumption was that the liberalization of the Indian economy has brought with it a change in the structural opportunities for women. Traditionally, women were not expected to have careers outside home, and their role was largely restricted to that of a homemaker. But urbanization and industrialization along with progressively greater access to education has opened up opportunities for women to work outside the home and to have independent careers. We made the assumption that the opening of the economy and exposure to other cultures would be reflected in the gender portrayals in the advertisements. If this were true, the number of Indian women portrayed in career roles in ads should show an increase from 1987 to 1997. We found that there was a drop in the number of women depicted in "domestic" roles by almost half, as expected. At the same time though, there was also a 25% drop in the frequency of women portrayed in career or occupational roles. The drop in the frequency of women in homemaker roles seems to have been absorbed by a similar increase in the frequency of women portrayed as fashion models (see Appendix, Table 7.7).

Next, the written copy that appeared in the advertisements was examined. Similar to the cultural cues, we created an index of items to study and compared the ad copy between 1987 and 1997. The frequency of ads where the copy refers to a woman's beauty went up by more than four times, and the number of times that the copy referred to health went up almost twice. References in the copy to losing weight as a way of staying healthy and references to weight and dieting went up between two to three times the numbers in 1987. This upward trend was also seen in references to skin complexion and skin color. Explicit references drawing comparisons between the model and the reader were made in 6.4% of the ads in 1987 and 33.1% of the ads in 1997. Lastly, the model in 0.8% of the ads in 1987 and 7.1% of the ads in 1997 endorsed the product (see Appendix, Table 7.8).

The increase in the coverage of beauty and health and the decrease in focus on food are in line with our assumption that thinness as an ideal value espoused in the West has also arrived in India. The data discussed in this section clearly convey several interesting, even startling occurrences in the Indian context. Cultural cues that have for long been considered a part of the Indian fabric are being replaced by more universal, Western cultural symbols. Even ideals in physical features are now being drawn in from the West. It would be no exaggeration to say that Indian advertising imagery has made some dramatic changes in the past decade or more. Ideals that were adhered to, even promoted in 1987 had been replaced with new ones in 1997.

Impact of Changing Media Content on Indian Audiences

Although peer pressure is the primary predictor of the drive for thinness among adolescents, internalization of media images could also be mediating the influence as well as having a direct influence on adult women's drive for thinness. This is borne out in the data from our focus groups conducted by the authors in Hyderabad, one of India's largest cities. Across the different groups, we found that there was a basic awareness, even an acceptance, of a growing thinness depicted in the media—possibly an outcome of the internalization of these media images.

Although women in both groups looked to the media as a guide to the world of beauty, the trend of thinner models and the association between being thin and being beautiful is perceived differently by the different groups of women—mediated largely by their personal backgrounds and the economic status of their families. Not surprisingly, young women from English-speaking backgrounds were most likely to experience these pressures for thinness and attributed these pressures to a large extent on the media they were exposed to.

"Thin is beautiful," said one participant. "Thinner you are, the more beautiful . . . it is considered to be the most perfect figure even if it isn't 36–24–36. The lesser it is the better it is here."

Participants also spoke about a shift in the role-models on matters related to beauty. The ideal beauties used to be movie actors, but over the past decade or so, they have been replaced by beauty fashion models and beauty pageant winners. Traditionally, actresses in India tended to be "full bodied," a comment on an earlier beauty ideal. But as one focus group participant told us "[such a body type] is looked down upon now." "Each film review makes it a point to say that [such actresses] have 'thunder thighs,' are too full, and must reduce."

Although the pressure for thinness may have been actively acknowledged by only a few in our groups, the participants unanimously attributed the construction of the new beauty within Indian culture to the media. As echoed in literature available in this area and in line with Bandura's hypothesis on vicarious learning of behaviors with positive associations, our focus group participants also spoke of the associations between the model's appearances and positive outcomes such as successful careers and families among others.

"[Media] project a lot of positive things about thinness. If you are thin, you are more confident, it helps in your career, and you can present yourself better. So that in itself is a very strong influence, more so than friends and parents."

Although perceptions of thinness-depicting media images may vary across the groups, equally noteworthy is the finding that the rules of the game have changed. Across groups, there was greater exposure to foreign magazines and television programming. Women today are conversant with global fashion trends and find themselves with very different benchmarks than existed prior to the country's economic liberalization.

DISCUSSION

This chapter is a first report of our research into the penetration of Western cultural formats across national borders and the impact of these imports on local professional practices and audiences. In this report, using gender portrayal and the conception of beauty as an exemplar, we examined the association between the increasing integration of the Indian economy with the world and the simultaneous change in the social construction of beauty as seen in the advertisements. The researchers specifically content-analyzed all advertisements containing women's images in three Indian magazines at two time-points, representing pre- and post-liberalization phases of the Indian economy. A wide range of variables were studied, so that each could be interpreted within the context of blurring cultural distinctions and "Westernization" of developing country audiences. Summarizing the trend in advertising and media images from the content analysis of the ads coupled with the preliminary trends in attitudes and behaviors as seen in our focus group discussions, one could argue in the direction of "homogenization of cultures" and "Westernization" of Third World audiences.

Although the case study presented uses data from the 1990s, the inflow of transnational organizations into India and the integration of the Indian economy with an increasingly "global" one have only increased since the period of the case study.

Further changes, since 1997, in permissible limits in foreign direct investment in a variety of industries such as telecom and construction are just a few cases in point. And as has been seen in the past, the inflow of transnational investment will most likely be accompanied by a subsequent inflow of globally used advertising and communication formats—further accentuating trends seen in the case study so far.

Even a brief glance across magazine stands in India today finds a far more "international" spread vis-à-vis a few years ago. Western women's and fashion magazines such as *Elle, Cosmopolitan,* and *Good Housekeeping* all have editions for the Indian consumers—yet another form of transfer of media professionalism and format as proposed by Golding (1977).

The large hype, the communication, and the money surrounding international beauty pageants and the more recent phenomenon of model searches have only further integrated the Indian glamour/beauty industry with that of the Western world. International pageants and beauty contests formats are being replicated on Indian television and media, bringing yet another dimension to the transfer of media professionalism as spoken about by Golding. Beauty may still remain in the eyes of the beholders; the beholders are perhaps all looking through the same eyes.

At this point however, we must emphasize that when we talk about "Westernization" or the "Americanization" of Third World audiences, we are talking more in terms of the exaggerated ideals of the United States portrayed by the media. In no way are we implying that these ideals form an accurate reflection of North American culture itself; rather as put forth by Schudson (1984), it is a "plane of reality" by itself.

Our study data show a definite movement from the locally conceived and culture-specific ideas of beauty towards a more standardized concept of beauty that originated in the West. Models are thinner and less voluptuous than they were even 10 years prior to the study period. Skin tones are lighter than they were pre-liberalization, and even physical features are more in line with those being flaunted in the West. In a study carried out by Simmonds et al. (1997), differences in body images for African American women and white women were studied in advertisements in magazine issues of 1996. They found that 17% of the models in *Cosmopolitan*, 26% of the models in *YM* and 13% of the models in *Ebony* had "thinner" bodies. Comparing that to data analyzed as part of the case study, we find that over a fifth of the Indian models in 1997 were categorized as thin, whereas the frequency of thin models in 1987 was only 1.9%. Similarly, only 0.3% to 1% of the models in the Simmonds et al. study were coded "obese." In our study, 1% of the models in 1997 were coded as obese compared with 1.9% in 1987. In both these cases, one can tell that the women's body size ideals portrayed in the advertisements were closer to the American representations as documented in the Simmonds et al. study than to the Indian representation of women's body size ten years prior in 1987 (see Appendix, Table 7.9).

Comparing the models' figures as coded in the two studies, once again one finds striking similarities between the Indian advertisements of 1997 and the American ads of 1996—more so than between the Indian advertisements of 1997 and 1987. Close to 15% of the Indian models in 1997 were coded as being "twiggy." The corresponding numbers in *Cosmopolitan, YM,* and *Ebony* were between 10% and 18%, whereas it was only 2.6% for the Indian ads of 1987.

One of the most instructive aspects of the results is the depiction of cultural cues that we had singled out as being identifying Indian characteristics. A drop in the number of models shown in Indian clothing, wearing a *bindi* or other such symbols of Indian culture are all indicative of a move away from the "Indian" and towards the "Western." In a case like that of toe rings that we had included as a cultural cue in our study, we found that none of the ads showed models wearing toe rings. By highlighting the greater correlation between the Indian ads of 1997 and the American ads of 1996 than those between the Indian ads of 1987 and 1997, we are not only putting forth the idea of cultural homogenization but are also underscoring the process by which this has come to be.

Previous studies such as Griffin et al. (1994) discussed the transfer of professional practices from the West to India, with specific reference to gender advertising. The case study presented not only corroborates the Griffin et al. study, rather it builds further on their inferences. In their study, Griffin et al. stated that advertising executives in India often use Western ads as prototypes for their own. Certainly, such an activity would result in ads similar in concept and layout to their Western counterparts. Given that this was the practice even prior to the entrance of transnational companies and foreign media outlets, it is certainly not surprising to see that the trend has only risen in the past few years, since economic liberalization of the country.

What needs to be highlighted is in our opinion the fact that the entrance of transnational companies has far-reaching consequences beyond just the economic ones. A company, like any other social organization, has rules and norms and an overall culture. As Golding (1977) observed, the transfer of professional practices through a direct transfer of a transnational company also is likely to lead to transfer of professional practices. Our argument is that the impact of economic liberalization is felt in areas such as the nation's culture as much as on the nation's economy. Transnational companies bring along with them their own advertisements, models, concepts, and layouts—

all pieces of Western culture. If beauty is a culture-specific notion, it is also most certainly a socially constructed one. With the entrance of the new players in the Indian economy and the resultant changes in the culture, the notion of beauty has also been changing over the past decade or so.

Going back to the data that we found on the growth in the number of foreign owned companies, this connection between the economic and cultural aspects of society becomes even more evident. Although one could possibly put forth counterarguments based on secular trends and the evolution of cultures, with changes as drastic as the ones we found in our study, such a proposition would probably explain much less than it would leave unexplained. Certainly, the relationship between the foreign media and the nature of the images found in them is more direct and in some ways intuitive as well. An impact on media images as a result of the entrance of foreign media should therefore come as less of a surprise.

Another indication of an increasing cultural blend between Indian and Western cultures is the intensified spotlight placed on international beauty pageants. One could argue that the increasing number of international beauty pageants that have been won by Indian contestants is yet another demonstration of transferred cultural standards; and that the positive reinforcements that the winners of these pageants receive only further deepens these cultural standards within the Indian psyche.

This study has drawn our attention to an issue that is of growing importance across the world—that of the media and their influence on audiences. It has also alerted us to the fact that media influences are not endemic to any one part of the world, but are indeed global. With the globalization of the media and close ties that are developing between the economies of different countries, one can expect to be witness to a lot more homogenization and blending of cultures. Viswanath and Zheng (2000) argue for a deeper examination of the nexus of relationship between "glamour and communication industry, a glamour-communication industry complex, and the impact of this mutually beneficial relationship on the intended and unintended audience." As major advertisers in women's magazines, the glamour industry composed of cosmetics and fashion apparel has been at the leading edge of fashion exports as well as in appropriating global cultural symbols to make fashion statements. A closer examination and product specific analyses do indeed show the critical role being played by the glamour-communication industry complex as one of the driving forces of globalization of local cultural formats in advertising and entertainment. A fuller understanding of the role of international advertising in globalization and its local impact hence requires a more holistic approach using political economy, structural functionalist, and cultural studies methods.

Further, our present research also clearly argues for expanding the construct of foreign media effects beyond individual-level analyses to analyses of institutional practices and products.

APPENDIX

Table 7.1.
Foreign Companies in India (by Country of Origin) in March of Each Given Year

COUNTRY/YEAR	1985	1990	1991	1992	1993	1994	1995
UK	106	130	131	131	137	141	153
USA	66	101	103	108	113	121	134
Japan	25	45	50	51	53	59	61
Germany	10	19	21	24	26	28	31
France	10	19	19	19	20	22	25
Hong Kong	1	12	15	16	17	18	19
Australia	–	7	8	9	10	11	17
Netherlands	4	7	8	8	9	12	15
Italy	–	12	12	13	13	13	14
Canada	–	7	7	7	7	8	11
Panama	1	9	9	9	9	9	9
Sweden	3	8	8	8	8	8	8
Others	68	93	98	104	107	115	122

Source: Indian Statistical Outline 1997–1998

Table 7.2.
Growth in Television and Cable TV Audiences from 1990 to 1997

YEAR		NUMBER OF HOUSEHOLDS ('000S)
1990	Estimated Households	38,834 (100%)
	TV Owning (before cable)	18,732 (48.2%)
1995	Estimated Households	44,856 (100%)
	TV Owning	27,016 (60.2%)
	Cable and Satellite households	9,266 (21%)
1997	Estimated Households	48,611 (100%)
	TV Owning	33,611 (69.1%)
	Cable and Satellite households	14,984 (30.8%)

Source: National Readership Surveys, 1990, 1995, 1997

Table 7.3
Cross-temporal Representation of Size and Weight of Models in Advertisements in Three Indian Magazines, in 1987 and 1997

SIZE AND WEIGHT OF MODEL	FREQUENCY % (N)	
	1987	1997
Thin/bony/scrawny	1.9 (5)	20.9 (73)
Normal	50.8 (135)	30.0 (105)
Full figured	9.8 (26)	5.1 (18)
Obese/overweight	1.9 (5)	0.6 (2)
Can't tell	43.4 (152)	35.7 (95)
Total number of ads	266	350

Chi-square = 68.75, d.f. = 4, p ≤.001

Table 7.4
Representation of the Model's Figure in Advertisements in Three Indian Magazines, in 1987 and 1997

MODEL'S FIGURE	FREQUENCY % (N)	
	1987	1997
Muscular	0.8 (2)	1.7 (6)
Voluptuous	16.2 (43)	7.7 (27)
Twiggy	2.6 (7)	14.9 (52)
Normal	10.2 (27)	15.4 (54)
Can't say	70.3 (187)	60.3 (211)
Total number of ads	266	350

Chi-square = 39.71, d.f. = 4, $p \leq .001$

Table 7.5
Frequency of Cultural Cues in Advertisements in Three Indian Magazines, in 1987 and 1997

CULTURAL CUES	FREQUENCY % (N) 1987	FREQUENCY % (N) 1997	SIGNIFICANCE AT P £ .05
Model is wearing glass bangles	7.1 (19)	3.7 (13)	$X^2 = 18.317$ d.f. $= 2, p \leq .001$
Model is wearing a *bindi*	33.8 (90)	9.1 (32)	$X^2 = 64.161$ d.f. $= 2, p \leq .001$
Model is in Indian clothing	43.2 (115)	15.1 (53)	$X^2 = 60.379$ d.f. $= 2, p \leq .001$
Model is wearing a *mangalsutra*	6.8 (18)	3.4 (12)	ns
Model is wearing toe rings	0	0	ns
Total number of ads	266	350	

Table 7.6
Media Images of Skin Tone of Models in Advertisements in Three Indian Magazines, in 1987 and 1997

SKIN TONE	FREQUENCY % (N) 1987	FREQUENCY % (N) 1997
Pale/anemic	0.8 (2)	3.4 (12)
White	5.6 (15)	10.3 (36)
Light skinned	39.5 (105)	56.6 (198)
Average, light brown	42.1 (112)	27.1 (95)
Dark skinned	9.8 (26)	1.4 (5)
Can't tell	2.3 (6)	1.1 (4)
Total number of ads	266	350

Chi-square $= 49.828$, d.f. $= 5, p \leq .001$

Table 7.7
Roles Played by the Model in Advertisements
in Three Indian Magazines, in 1987 and 1997

	FREQUENCY % (N)	
ROLE	1987	1997
Domestic role	39.5 (105)	20.9 (71)
Career/occupational	4.1 (11)	2.9 (10)
Fashion model	38.7 (103)	56.0 (196)
Can't say	17.7 (47)	20.9 (73)
Total number of ads	266	350

Chi-square = 30.284, d.f. = 3, $p \leq$ .001

Table 7.8
Copy References in Ads in Three
Indian Magazines, in 1987 and 1997

	FREQUENCY IN % (N)		SIGNIFICANCE
COPY REFERS TO	1987	1997	at $p \leq$ .05
Woman's beauty	7.5 (20)	31.7 (111)	X^2 = 52.843, d.f. =1, $p \leq$ .001
Health	2.3 (6)	4.3 (15)	Ns
Weight or diet	0.8 (2)	2.0 (7)	Ns
Losing weight to remain healthy	0.4 (1)	1.4 (5)	Ns
Skin complexion	4.9 (13)	16.3 (57)	X^2 = 19.496, d.f. =1, $p \leq$ .001
Skin color	0.8 (2)	2.9 (10)	Ns
Relationship with man	1.1 (3)	5.7 (20)	X^2 = 8.845, d.f. =1, $p \leq$ .05
Comparison of reader to model	6.4 (17)	33.1 (116)	X^2 = 63.891, d.f. =1, $p \leq$ .001
Model's endorsement of product	0.8 (2)	7.1 (25)	X^2 = 14.729, d.f. =1, $p \leq$ .001

Table 7.9
Comparison of the Portrayal of Body Images
in Advertisements in American and Indian Women's
Magazines, 1996 and 1997

SIZE AND WEIGHT OF THE MODEL	AMERICAN MAGAZINES Frequency %	INDIAN MAGAZINES Frequency %
Thin/bony/scrawny	18	20.9
Slender/normal	52.0 ("slender")	30.0 ("normal")
Full figured	2.8	5.1
Obese/overweight	0.6	0.6
Can't tell	27	35.7
Total number of ads	1142	350

REFERENCES

Anderson, A. E., & DiDomenico, L. (1992). Diet vs. shape content of popular male and female magazines from Simmon's study of media and markets. *International Journal of Eating Disorders, 11*(3), 283–287.

Bandura A. (2002). Social cognitive theory of mass communication. In J. Bryant & D. Zillmann (Eds.), *Media effects: Advances in theory and research* (pp. 61-90). Hillsdale, NJ: Erlbaum.

Bryant, J., & Zillmann, D. (Eds.). (2002). *Media effects: Advances in theory and research*. Mahwah, NJ: Erlbaum.

Cusumano, D. L., & Thompson, J. K. (1997). Body image and body shape ideals in magazines, exposure, awareness and internalization. *Sex Roles, 37*(9–10), 701–721.

Field, A. E., Cheung, L., Wolf, A. M., Herzog, D. B., Gortmaker, S. L., & Colditz, G. A. (1999, March). Exposure to mass media and weight concerns among girls. *Pediatrics, 103*(3), E36.

Fiss, P. C., & Hirsch, P. M. (2005). The discourse of globalization: Framing and sensemaking of an emerging concept. *American Sociological Review, 70*(1), 29–52.

Gerbner, G., Gross, L., Morgan, M., Signorielli, N., & Shanahan, J. (2002). Growing up with television: Cultivation process. In J. Bryant & D. Zillmann (Eds.), *Media effects: Advances in theory and research*. Mahwah, NJ: Erlbaum.

Goffman, E. (1987). *Gender advertisements*. New York: Harper Torchbooks.

Golding, P. (1977). Media professionalism in the Third World: The transfer of an ideology. In J. Curran, M. Gurevitch, & J. Woollacott (Eds.), *Mass communication and society* (pp. 291–308). Beverly Hills, CA: Sage.

Griffin, M., Viswanath, K., & Schwartz, D. (1994). Gender advertising in United States and India—Exporting cultural stereotypes. *Media Culture and Society,* *16*(3), 487–507.

Holsti, O. R. (1964). Content analysis for social sciences and humanities. In G. H. Stempel III & B. Westley (Eds.), *Research methods in mass communication.* Englewood Cliffs, NJ: Prentice-Hall.

Hovland, R., & Wilcox, G. B. (Eds.). (1989). *Advertising in society: Classic and contemporary readings on advertising's role in society* (pp. 277–297). Lincolnwood, IL: NTC Business Books.

Iyengar, S., & Kinder, D. R. (1987). *News that matters: Television and American opinion.* Chicago: University of Chicago Press.

Jamieson, K. H., & Campbell, K. K. (1992). *Interplay of influence: News, advertising, politics, and the mass media* (pp. 252–292). Belmont, CA: Wadsworth.

Lee, C. C. (1982). *Media imperialism reconsidered.* Beverly Hills, CA: Sage.

Leiss, W., Kline, S., & Jhally, S. (1986). *Social communication in advertising.* Toronto: Methuen.

Myers, P. N., & Biocca, F. A. (1992). The elastic body image: The effect of television advertising and programming on body image distortions in young women. *Journal of Communication, 42*(3), 108–133.

Schudson, M. (1984). *Advertising, the uneasy persuasion.* New York: Basic Books.

Silverstein, B., Perdue, L., Peterson, B., & Kelly, E. (1986). The role of mass media in promoting a thin standard of bodily attractiveness for women. *Sex Roles, 14,* 519–532.

Simmonds, B., Urbano, K., Ogilvy, C., & Viswanath, K. (1997). *Black and White: Differences in body images in advertisements for African-American and White women.* Paper presented at the annual conference of the Association for Education in Journalism and Mass Communication, Chicago, July 31–August 2.

Sypeck, M. F., Gray, J. J., & Ahrens, A. H. (2004). No longer a pretty face: Fashion magazines' depiction of ideal female beauty from 1959 to 1999. *International Journal of Eating Disorders, 36*(3), 342–347.

Tichenor, P. J., Donohue, G. A., & Olien, C. N. (1980). *Community conflict and the press.* Beverly Hills, CA: Sage.

Turner, S. L., Hamilton, H., & Jacobs, M. (1997). The influence of fashion magazines on the body image satisfaction of college women: An explanatory analysis. *Adolescence, 32*(127), 603–614.

Ulrich. (1999). Ovid Technologies field Guide. Ulrich's™ International Periodicals Directory (ULRI). Retrieved from http://ovid.gwdg.de/ovidweb/fldguide/ulrich.htm.

Viswanath, K., & Balasubramanian, K. (2000). *Advertising, body images and implications for public health: A comparative analysis of American and Indian women's magazines.* Paper presented at the annual Kentucky Conference on Health Communication, University of Kentucky, Lexington, KY, April 13–15.

Viswanath K., & Demers D. (1999). Mass media from a macrosocial perspective. In D. Demers & K. Viswanath (Eds.), *Mass media, social control and social change: A macrosocial perspective.* Ames: Iowa State University Press.

Viswanath, K., & Karan, K. (2000). India. In S. Guanaratne (Ed.), *Media in Asia.* New Delhi: Sage.

Viswanath K., & Zheng L. (2000). International advertising. In W. B. Gudykunst & B. Mody (Eds.), *Handbook of international and intercultural communication* (3rd ed.). Thousand Oaks, CA: Sage.

Wiseman, C. V., Gray, J. J., Mosimann, J. E., & Ahrens, A. H. (1992). Cultural expectations of thinness in women: An update. *International Journal of Eating Disorders, 11*(1), 85–89.

Zucker, A. N., Harrell, Z. A., Miner-Rubino, K., Stewart, A. J., Pomerleau, C. S., & Boyd, C. J. (2001). Smoking in college women: The role of thinness pressures, media exposure, and critical consciousness. *Psychology of Women Quarterly, 25,* 233–241.

8

REPRESENTATION OF PAKISTANI WOMEN IN THE MEDIA

Does Presence Mean Power?

Siddiqua Ovais

Pakistan, as an Islamic state, is becoming characterized as a nation of fanatics: uncaring of human rights, intolerant of differing beliefs, and abusive of its women. Around the world, the stereotypical view of Pakistani women is adding to the increasingly universal vision of Muslim women everywhere as a veiled and subdued, homogenous block.

Although it is true that Islam is a unifying factor for Muslims worldwide, and true that a majority of Muslim societies are patriarchal, these by no means paint the whole picture. This view ignores the specifics of region and cultural traditions. In Pakistan's case, the media have been partially responsible for a limited representation of women that reinforces the role of women as subservient caregivers and homemakers

Hampered though they are by traditions and laws that militate against their independence, Pakistani women are negotiating for space and autonomy and are organizing politically and socially to redefine the parameters of their existence. This process has recently been given the added impetus of two significant changes: the development of a National Plan of Action for Women and the liberalization of the media in Pakistan.

This means that while government laws and regulations are changing to facilitate working women, the media are also opening up and granting more space and freedom to women. Not so long ago, Pakistani women were instructed to appear with their heads covered on national television. Now, the shift to showing young girls dressed in Western attire may not automatically signal a change in attitudes, but it is an indication that society is becoming more tolerant of its young and is prepared to grant a greater visibility and say to its women.

Around the globalizing world, cultural homogenization is prompting the reassertion of regional identities and the preservation of tradition. The internal conflict between globalization and localization are at their most pronounced in Pakistan today, as the country seeks acceptance by the international community as a progressive state

During its 57-year history Pakistan has known little political stability, and it is also against this backdrop that the women of Pakistan are struggling to be seen and heard. I hope that this study of the images of women in the media is timely and that it will help to lift the veil off the women of Pakistan.

BACKGROUND

The Significance of Islam for Pakistani Women

"Religion as culture has always been an important element in the identity of Muslims in their varied regional settings. But there has never been any agreement on religion as political ideology" (Bose & Jalal, 2004, p. 159). Pakistan was created in the name of religion, and Islam has had an undeniable influence on its politics.

It was under the banner of Islam that Muslim women took to the streets in support of an independent Islamic Pakistan. Ironically, once independence had been achieved, it was also in the name of religion that women were sent back to the confines of their homes. When the religious right started gaining strength in Pakistan the public appearance and presence of women became the target of discussion giving the orthodox section of society a "carte blanche to become self-styled moralists" (Mumtaz & Shaheed, 1987, p. 17).

Implications of Veiling in Pakistan

"Islamic clothing affects Islamic thinking and vice versa. As the Quran teaches modesty for both men and women, clothes are meant to emphasize modesty and dignity both in men and in women" (Ahmed, 1999, p. 159). However it was only women's clothing that became the target of debate in a 1978–88 drive for Islamization. Directives passed in 1980 and 1982 made the *chador* (a complete body covering used by orthodox Muslim women to veil their heads and bodies, while leaving the face visible) compulsory for all women government employees and later, for all women's colleges that came under the jurisdiction of the Federal Government. This created an atmosphere "whereby all males became the judge of a woman's modesty and status in society" (Mumtaz & Shaheed, 1987, p. 81). Although those directly affected by this policy were largely women working in government departments (which included the media), many other women also observed the practice of head covering during this period. On the one hand, this politicization of dress was a by-product of the politicization of Islam, while on the other, it was symbolic of a move in Pakistani society to look toward practices in Iran and the Middle East to lend legitimacy to Pakistan as an Islamic republic.

While today the practice of veiling is largely a matter of personal choice, the recent resurgence of the *hijab* (a veil or scarf that completely covers the hair) can be read, in Pakistan as elsewhere, as a reaction to the heightened pace of globalization. The hijab is simultaneously "a fashionable and recognizable symbol of Muslim identity," a way of saying, "this is where I stand and I am proud of it" (Ahmed, 1999, p. 161).

At present, the most popular veil in urban Pakistan is the dupatta, a long, scarf-like cloth worn with the *shalwar kameez* (a long shirt and trousers suit). It normally lies across the shoulders and can be used as a head covering if circumstances require. However as suggested in Mumtaz and Shaheed, (1987), in urban areas the dupatta is becoming more of a fashion accessory than a symbol of modesty.

PORTRAYAL OF WOMEN IN PAKISTANI MEDIA

Stereotyping the Pakistani Woman

The Pakistan media generally present the ideal Pakistani woman as meek, submissive, caring of her family, and happy to be confined to the home. At the same time, an overwhelmingly negative image of working women has been drummed into the Pakistani psyche. The conventional wisdom is that allowing women to work outside the home results in the break up of families, neglected children, and extramarital affairs. Historically, the only women able to avoid this stereotype were widows or spinsters forced from their homes to search for a livelihood (Asian Development Bank, 2000).

However, in the 1980s, more and more women started seeking employment, and the numbers of women employed in the media peaked. Ironically, it was during this period that the media were most disparaging of working women, upholding the traditional roles of women as mothers and daughters while debasing the status of women professionals by airing drama serials and plays in which working women were portrayed as the cause of neglected households and errant children.

With respect to reporting women's issues, the press has been accused of adopting a conventional approach, praising submissiveness as a virtue and denouncing women's attempts at independence. Simply by reporting crimes against women in a particular way, journalists appear to be justifying the crime and hence perpetuating traditions of male hegemony. Such misrepresentations are also attributed to the domination of males employed in the Urdu-language press, which reaches almost 80% of the newspaper market. "They have a somewhat conformist approach towards women's issues" (Ansari, 2001, p. 93). Ansari says, "Many women are denied jobs in the Urdu-language newspapers. Those who are hired are hounded by the male staff, often to the extent that they decide to quit their jobs" (p. 93). A similar trend can be observed in the vernacular language press, which thrives on sensationalism. Incidents involving women therefore become highly publicized with attention to sordid details as a means of attracting attention and increasing readership. Also, while the role of the career woman is as yet to find its place in the media, the idea of the stay-at-home husband is wholly alien to the Pakistani psyche (Ansari, 2001).

An article in the *Dawn*, a local daily newspaper, reported on a split in opinion among the Pakistani people regarding images of women in the media. While a survey conducted by the United Nations Development Program (UNDP) claimed that people would like to see women projected in bold and assertive roles, another study conducted by an advertising agency maintained that a majority of the informants favored some form of media censorship that would reflect social norms (Ilahi, 2001). The article concludes that the audience was basically averse to both over-glamorization and extreme submissiveness in the portrayal of women. The abovementioned surveys were conducted as part of a project, *Portrayal of Women in Media*, initiated by the UNDP in collaboration with Pakistan Television. The study sought to facilitate a positive, balanced, and diverse image of women in media, the objective being female empowerment in every context (Ilahi, 2001). The project was the first of its kind in Pakistan.

The Representation of Women in Pakistan Advertising

Around 1980, the government issued circulars to Pakistan television concerning women and advertisements. "Ostensibly aimed at ensuring that no attempt is made to exploit the fair sex for commercial purposes, these directives eliminated women from the commercials advertising products having little or no relevance to women" (Mumtaz & Shaheed, 1987, p. 81). According to the authors, the intention of the government was not so much to protect the women as it was to prescribe the role thought most appropriate for women. This was to be achieved mainly by portraying women as homemakers and users of household items. "This directive was soon followed by another, forbidding female models to appear for more than 25% of the allotted time for a commercial" (Mumtaz & Shaheed, 1987, p. 81).

In 1997, advertisers were told that commercials should be "simple and congruous with the Islamic values and culture. . . . Ladies projected in TV commercials should wear full national dress. Immodest or indecent dresses exhibiting body contours are not allowed" (Barraclough, 2001, p. 233). Accordingly, advertisements that featured images of women tossing their hair to promote shampoo and smiling seductively to sell toothpaste were prohibited, and international brands such as *Sunsilk* and *Close-Up* had their advertisements banned. In contrast to the continuing airing of foreign shows and advertisements on cable television, these bans appeared hypocritical and reactionary. "In the face of wider exposure to more permissive foreign media, the Pakistani government was not merely holding its ground, it was in fact becoming more conservative" (Barraclough, 2001, p. 234).

While advertisements on state television, Pakistan Television (PTV), are governed by the PTV's Code of Advertising Standards and Practice, programming content on cable TV networks is regulated by the Pakistan Electronic Media Regulatory Authority (PEMRA). However, these rules also require that "the advertisements shall conform to the TV Code of Advertising Standards and Practices in Pakistan" (PEMRA Rules, 2002). The PTV's Code of Advertising Standards and Practice in relation to women states that:

- Advertisements for products/services that have no relevance to women should not feature any female model; products/services exclusively meant for the fair sex can project female models but the main emphasis of the commercial should be on the product rather than on the model.
- Advertisements of products/services that are of common use by both the sexes can also feature females to a limited extent; unnecessary projection should be avoided.

Also to be avoided:

- Women in tight costumes, sleeveless and low-cut outfits exhibiting body contours. Scenes of men and women undressing and their indecent movements; display of human figure in the nude (*Orient Blue Book*, 2002, pp. 30, 31).

STEPS TOWARDS IMPROVING THE
REPRESENTATION OF WOMEN

To date, there are about 19 listed women's groups in Pakistan—working in areas of women's rights, social and economic progress, providing legal aid and adequate representation in the government. Although many groups are often criticized for their elitist constitution and their distance from the realities of the majority of Pakistani women, it is due to the combined efforts of these organizations that the representation of women in government has risen to 33%, the National Policy for Development and Empowerment of Women has been formulated, and the first private channel for women has been launched on the GEO television cable network.

Currently, women are becoming more visible in managerial positions in the media and elsewhere. For instance, the director of programs for Pakistan Television is a woman, and so is the CEO of Lever Brothers in Pakistan—the first time in this country's history that a woman has headed a multinational corporation (see Appendix B, Table 8.1). Moreover, contrary to the traditional concepts of women as hosts of fashion and domestic programs, a significant number of women are now conducting current affairs programs and discussing political issues in the media.

National Policy for Development and Empowerment
of Women

In 2004, the first-ever National Policy for Development and Empowerment of Women was formulated. Its aims and objectives are to:

- Remove inequities and imbalances in all sectors of socioeconomic development and to ensure women's equal access to all development benefits and social services;
- Ensure the participation of women as equal partners in national development and decision-making processes in the community and society;
- Ensure the full participation of women in all political processes and to enhance women's representation in all elective bodies;
- Safeguard and ensure the protection of women's human rights including economic, legal, political, and social rights, especially the rights of minority women, rural and poor women, girls and women with disabilities, elderly women, and women in vulnerable circumstances and situations;

- Provide women and girls access to quality health care services and all other prerequisites to enjoying full health, including reproductive and mental health;
- Expeditiously and substantially enhance women's literacy rates, improve attainment levels of girls and women at all levels of education (both academic and professional) to reduce the gender gap, and to reorient existing curricula by making them gender sensitive;
- Provide equality of opportunity and to create space for women to realize their full potential.

Additionally, specific areas of the policy address issues of discrimination and harassment; the role of the media as a means of information, education, and communication on women's issues; and a positive portrayal of women in all media. In addition, the policy is aimed at initiating awareness campaigns—especially in the media and in schools through textbooks—to promote the positive benefits of an equal sharing of responsibilities, decision making, and power between women and men inside and outside the home with focus on gender-sensitive men and caring fathers and husbands ("National Policy," 2004).

CONTENT ANALYSIS OF WOMEN'S MAGAZINE ADVERTISEMENTS

The fact that in Pakistan, women's magazines account for 40% of the total magazine market gives an indication of their significance to Pakistani society. For this study, six issues of six different titles of women's magazines were selected to represent a cross-section of the different media available to each stratum of society. Thus, a total of 36 magazines comprised the sample. Although advertisements in women's magazines are a good means of detecting emerging, nontraditional roles of women, they are also a reflection of the current norms of society. To be resonant with their target audience, advertisements must, for the most part, reflect current cultural values.

Based on the above premise, a content analysis was conducted of advertisements in women's magazines targeting the three basic strata of society: the lower, primarily Urdu-speaking groups, as well as the middle- and the upper income groups. Two titles representing each stratum were selected on the basis of popularity and pricing. The Urdu magazines, *She* and *Pakeeza*, priced at Rs.35 (US $0.59) each, are popular among the lower income groups. (*She* is also published in an English-language edition that differs in content and caters to English reading audiences.) *She* is the first news mag-

azine for women in Urdu, and *Pakeeza* is popular among the types of magazines commonly known as "digests" that feature mainly serials and short
stories.

Popular English-language magazines are *She* (English) and *Women's
Own*. Whereas *She* is the largest selling English-language monthly, *Women's
Own* claims to cover "the complete woman." They are priced at Rs.80 and
Rs.70 (US $1.34 and $1.17) respectively and appeal to the middle- and upper
middle classes. Although the language may restrict readership, these magazines are nevertheless popular because their fashion spreads appeal to
women of all classes.

Social Pages and *Visage*, representing the last category of fashion/
lifestyle magazines, cater mainly to women from higher income groups.
These publications are also in the English language and are priced at Rs.150
and Rs.215 (US $2.50 and $3.60) respectively.

CONTENT ANALYSIS OF TELEVISION
ADVERTISEMENTS

For this study, GEO, a private satellite channel, was contrasted with
Pakistan Television, the state-owned channel. GEO was selected from
among other private channels because its profile of news, entertainment, and
education closely matches that of Pakistan Television. GEO started transmission on October 1, 2002, and has the widest distribution on cable systems in Pakistan ("Facts about GEO," 2005). Pakistan Television, the government network, on the other hand, beamed its first transmission on
November 26, 1964, and enjoyed its status as the broadcasting monopoly
until the recent liberalization.

Advertisements that aired during prime time (8–9 pm) on three consec-
utive days on both the channels were recorded. Because the study concerned
the roles of women, advertisements showing only children or men were
excluded from the sample. Repeated advertisements were, however, included because frequency is part of advertising strategy and adds to the effectiveness of message delivery.

CODING PROCEDURE

The methodology for the study is adapted from the research conducted by
Siu and Au (1997) on the representation of women in advertisements in
China and Singapore. Certain similarities in cultural values, such as the roles

of women, which are wholly defined by their relations to men (Siu & Au, 1997), and the relationship between senior and junior members of society make their study an appropriate reference point for my study.

However, because my study was concerned with the role of women per se, the roles of men in these advertisements and commercials were studied only insofar as they determined the male/female relationship. Five variables were analyzed for each advertisement or commercial: type of product, role of woman, dress code of woman, presence of man, and the woman's relationship with the man. Seven roles were determined for the female: mother, wife/girlfriend, friend, career woman, celebrity, decorative, and Western model. A detailed explanation of the variables is given in Appendix A.

For magazine ads, the unit of analysis was restricted to advertisements of one or more full pages, containing at least one woman. The coding criteria for classifying roles depicted in the ads required that both the face and some part of the model's dress or figure be shown in the ad. Hence, advertisements featuring only a face and neck were not included in the study. In advertisements where more than one woman was present, the dominant model was coded. The clothing of women was also coded according to the presence or absence of the dupatta, which acts as an indicator of traditional or modern dress. Based on the given criteria, a total of 606 advertisements were coded.

For television, commercials featuring adult female characters with an on-camera appearance of three seconds and/or at least one line of dialogue were coded. In advertisements where more than one woman was present, the woman playing the dominant role was coded. A total of 104 advertisements were recorded for PTV, and 102 were recorded for GEO.

RESEARCH FINDINGS

Magazine Advertisements

A total of 625 identifiable roles for women were coded in the 606 advertisements from the 36 magazines. The apparent discrepancy is due to some ads having a woman playing more than one role, such as both wife and mother. Of these categories, decorative appeared as the dominant role of women (50%) and the role of the career woman appeared as least popular (1%). The presence of women as wives/girlfriends and as mothers were at par (14%) with one another. Although the occurrence of both women's roles was more or less equal across the magazines, the only notable difference was in the category of mother–that role was observed almost twice as many times in Urdu-language magazines (21%) as in English-language magazines (11%) (see Appendix B, Table 8.2).

Products in Magazine Advertisements. The most advertised products in the women's magazines were beauty and personal care products (35%), and the category of services were the least advertised (4%) (See Appendix B, Table 8.3). This result is somewhat to be expected, given that the decorative role for women predominated. The second most popular product, food (23%), also coincides with the next most observed role for women—that of the wife.

Relationship between Men and Women. As shown in Table 8.4 (Appendix B), the total number of advertisements portraying a male was 102, which is 17% of the total number of advertisements. With regard to male presence and their relationship with women in the ads, I found that when a male was present, it was usually in the role of a husband or boyfriend. It is, however, important to note that the male/female relationship in these advertisements was mainly one of equality (85%). I only saw the concept of subservience or waiting on the husband being represented on three occasions (3%), and I saw that the image of a woman being waited on only occurred once. However, in the latter case, the advertisement was of foreign origin and portrayed a Western model.

Women's Clothing in Ads. The relatively small difference in figures for the presence (49%) and absence (43%) of the dupatta seem to complement the view expressed earlier regarding the function of the dupatta—that of a fashion accessory rather than as a symbol of modesty (see Appendix B, Table 8.5). In none of the cases is the dupatta used as head covering; it was mainly shown around the neck or over the shoulder. In advertisements for clothing, it is usually draped to form the background (3%) while part of it lies in the model's hand or in her lap, giving it the status of a prop. The findings also indicate the rising trend of modern or Western forms of clothing where the dupatta plays no part. A comparison of magazines, however, reveals a greater presence of the dupatta in Urdu magazines (62%) as compared to English magazines (42%), which can be attributed to the different sociocultural composition of the readerships in each magazine.

Male Presence vis-à-vis the Presence of the Dupatta. It is also important to note that when the sample was coded for male and female couples, the presence or absence of the dupatta was significant. Out of a total of 102 advertisements where a male presence was recorded, the presence of the dupatta (61%) was significantly higher than its absence (36%). This seems to indicate that in her role as wife and mother of the family—specifically with a male present—the preferred dress code for women is still more or less traditional.

TV Advertisements

The role of the woman as wife/girlfriend leads in both PTV (47.1%) and GEO (49%), whereas the role of the mother is far more prevalent on PTV (37.5%) as compared to GEO (12.7%). In her role as wife/mother the woman is mostly seen advertising food/beverages and domestic appliances, in accordance with her accepted role as expert in the house and related issues (see Appendix B, Table 8.6).

The role of the career woman scores a little above the celebrity role on PTV (6.7%), whereas on GEO the presence (2.9%) is just above the Western model category. Where the woman does appear in this role, it is usually as a healthcare professional.

A study of the commercials on PTV and GEO reveals that whereas food and beverages are the most advertised of all products on PTV (34.6%), domestic appliances/furnishing is the leading category on GEO (36.3%). It is interesting to note that advertisements for domestic appliances/furnishings were completely absent from the PTV commercials in the study sample. Another category absent from the PTV sample is that of automobiles. Food and beverage follows as a close second on GEO (31.4%). Beauty and personal care products have a greater presence on PTV (26%) than on GEO (4.9%). Completely absent from GEO were household cleaning products. Institutional/public service advertising was also found more frequently on PTV (11.8%) than on GEO (2%). (See Appendix B. Table 8-7).

Relationship between Males and Females in Television Commercials. The presence of males in commercials is observed as 52.8% for PTV and 52% for GEO (see Appendix B, Table 8.8). The relationship with females was recorded as being close to equal in 80% and 86.8% of the commercials on PTV and GEO respectively. In only one case was a serving role observed.

DISCUSSION AND CONCLUSIONS

Dominant Roles for Women

From my analysis of the magazine advertisements and television commercials, it is apparent that the roles for women, as represented in Pakistan magazine advertisements, have not undergone a major change but largely conform to the historical and cultural roles women play as wives and mothers. This is primarily due to the fact that women do indeed occupy a very small portion of a labor force that is dominated by men. However, this trend does not appear to be universal across the media, with the state television portraying women as mothers the most and magazines the least.

Decorative Role of Women in Magazines

The predominance of the role of decorative female in magazine advertisements is an indication of the reach of the medium and its main target audience. Because the products advertised in the women's magazines were for personal care and women's clothing items, the focus is on a woman's appearance. However, although the Pakistani woman is shown in ads in a decorative role, she stops short of becoming a sex symbol mainly due to the social and cultural norms that form the basis of Pakistani society.

Role of Woman as Homemaker on Television

The role of woman as wife/mother is more frequently portrayed on PTV than on GEO. Pakistan Television still enjoys the largest reach across all of Pakistan, whereas GEO, a relatively new satellite channel, has found an audience mainly in the urban areas. This is perhaps the main reason why high-end domestic appliances are conspicuous by their absence from PTV and are found in the sample recorded for GEO Television. The nature of advertisements on the two channels has obviously dictated the dominant roles for women in these media. GEO thus has a higher ratio of housewives followed by women in decorative roles in advertising mainly food/beverage and domestic appliances. PTV, on the other hand, has to identify with rural/urban, lower- and lower middle-class audiences. As a result, PTV ran ads for low-end products such as food/beverages and personal care. These occupied the largest share of advertising when the model's role was predominantly as mother or housewife. A major factor responsible for the dominance of this role has cultural underpinnings; the mother is a highly revered figure in Pakistani society. Also as far as the PTV is concerned there is a definite effort at educating the woman—especially the rural woman—regarding her rights as a mother and a wife.

The role of the career woman is still largely absent from the advertising scene in Pakistan, which is a reflection of her absence from these real-life roles. It is apparent from my analysis and through discussions with experts that the working woman still forms a very low proportion of the women in Pakistan. Consequently, the depiction of a woman in an office setting would probably find little appeal with the audience. In the few instances when a career woman has been identified, it was primarily in the role of a doctor.

The only digression from this has been the portrayal on television of women as nurses—generally regarded as an inferior occupation that is often relegated to women. These commercials point to a concerted effort on the part of the government to encourage women to enter these professions while educating the society to look upon them with greater respect. However, although the role of the working woman in an office setting is not yet very common, certain lifestyle products aimed at saving time do appear to be directed at women juggling homes, careers, and children.

Taking into account the source and the recipient of advertising messages, it can be said that advertisers and consumers have a significant role to play in determining the presence and role of women in advertisements. In most cases, executives in advertising and marketing are men; consequently, it is male attitudes and views that determine how women are represented. The dominance of the decorative role for women, therefore, is somewhat hypocritical in a society that seeks to hide its women while at the same time failing to resist the temptation to exploit them when there is a possibility of economic gain.

But is worth noting that women seem to accept themselves in these roles. Judging by the popularity of women's magazines, it is reasonable to assume that women are comfortable with their contents as well as with the images they portray. Hence, as long as women continue to view themselves within the parameters of these prescribed roles, little change can be expected at the societal level.

Dress Code for Women

In my discussions with advertising and media personnel, they agreed that trendy, Western clothes are seldom worn by Pakistani women in real life. However, my analysis of the dress styles in the sample magazine advertisements shows that this is not the case in ads: The number of women shown in modern attire is almost equal to those in traditional wear, and the dupatta is fast being depicted as a fashion accessory rather than as a religious garment. In some cases, women are seen clothed in jeans or trousers, in sleeveless tops, and in some cases even in skirts. Again, I observed that the presence of the dupatta was more frequent in Urdu-language than in English-language magazines. It is also most frequently seen when male models were present in the ads. The latter situation can be viewed as emphasizing the status accorded to the dupatta as a symbol of modesty.

The conflicting desire to modernize at one level and the resurgence of the hijab on the other are undeniable effects of globalization. Added to this is the liberalization of the media, which have introduced Pakistanis to attitudes and practices that were hitherto considered alien. Although an obvious change wrought by the opening up of the media is the increased frequency of women appearing on screen in modern clothing, more importantly, this change has paved the way for the improved representation of women in Pakistan. Discussions of areas previously considered taboo, the setting up of a private TV channel dedicated to women's affairs, and women entering male-dominated areas on and off camera are among the indications that Pakistan society is prepared to give a bigger say to its women. Although, acting alone, the media cannot be expected to effect societal change, they can cause desensitization, which prepares the audience to accept more liberalized portrayals of women.

Although the issue of women's clothing may appear to be merely a cosmetic one, rules about dress are indicative of the way men wield power in the lives of women. Official dictates can mold women in roles "most suitable" for them, as was the case during the presidency of General Zia (1978–88). This apparently simple issue encapsulates the way women are perceived and discussed in society. Simply by limiting their appearance in public, society is able to disregard women's rights as individuals: The right to be heard derives from the right to be seen.

Equality in Male/Female Relationships

The way the media depict women in the company of men is constrained by social tradition. Commercial sense checks the extent to which advertising can push these limits: The representations must not offend society at large. This analysis of advertisements reveals that when men are present, the male-female relationship is primarily one of equality. Images of women being subservient to men are almost negligible. This seems to reflect the fact that although women are not yet ready to see themselves outside certain prescribed roles, there is some desire for equality.

Men are more frequently depicted with women on television than in magazines. State television, especially, promotes a feeling of equality between the sexes. This is apparent in family planning advertisements. Although such advertisements used to be directed mainly to women, the government has finally recognized that Pakistani society accords immense decision-making power to the male, and through him to his parents—especially his mother. In such cases, it is important for family planning issues to be recommended by a woman in authority, such as a doctor or a mother-in-law whose word holds great weight in rural areas and among lower and lower middle strata. Family planning commercials are now aimed at educating husbands and in-laws. So, the approach is now more towards persuading society rather than individuals. As a result, these commercials have a greater chance of bearing positive results.

Empowerment of Women

Although my study of advertisements did not reveal any depictions of new, unconventional, or modern roles for women, it did bring to light the significance of educated and aware women in role portrayals. Pakistani aspirational advertising encourages women in the lower strata of society to emulate these images and hence encourages them to move towards a better quality of life. Although this change is governed by the resources available to a woman, awareness of her rights as an individual is a step towards improving her lot in life.

The concept of women's empowerment is thus emerging in Pakistan, albeit in roles deemed suitable for them. Importantly, government communication specifically targeted to rural and lower- and lower middle-class women, is simultaneously heightening women's awareness of their rights and rendering society sensitive to their needs.

In conclusion, it is important to remember that the current states of both government and the newly liberalized media are still in an early phase of development, whereas it takes decades for social change to come about. These changes are taking place against a historical background of political instability that has slowed the development of social structures and institutions able to protect the rights of individuals—especially women.

Although advertisements may be good indicators of the stereotypes that exist in Pakistani society, they are less accurate indicators of divergent and emerging roles. Although working women have not made a significant impact on the official figures for the labor force of Pakistan, there is some evidence that an upward trend is taking place in the urban centers of the country. This being the case, a more accurate study of changes in the roles of women should be possible by analyzing local television shows where nontraditional roles of women are more likely to be present. This would be a way to take this study a step further, in that it would be possible to break down the roles of women in urban and rural areas; and it would allow for a focus on the largely ignored middle-class working woman—whose significant economic contributions still await recognition.

APPENDIX A

CODING MANUAL FOR ADVERTISEMENTS

1a. Product Categories Advertised in Magazines

1. Beauty and personal care—all kinds of cosmetics, perfumes, soaps, creams, hair/skin care, slimming, and beauty services
2. Women's clothing—all varieties of traditional and modern clothes
3. Women's accessories—including handbags, shoes, jewelry, watches
4. Food and food products—fast food, spices, beverages, health drinks
5. Pharmaceutical products—sanitary napkins, general drugs for family, slimming pills, and so on
6. Home furnishings/domestic appliances—refrigerators, air conditioners, washing machines, mobile phones, bedding, and home décor
7. Services—Credit cards, calling cards, banking services, internet services, airline, hotels
8. Other

1b. Product Categories Advertised on Television

1. Beauty and personal care—cosmetics, perfumes, soaps, creams, hair/skin care, slimming, and beauty services
2. Household cleaning products—soap detergents for laundry, dishwashing, etc.
3. Food and food products—fast food, spices, beverages, health drinks
4. Pharmaceutical products—general drugs for family, slimming pills, family planning pills, etc.
5. Domestic appliances/home furnishings—refrigerators, air-conditioners, washing machines, mobile phones, bedding, and home décor.

Automobiles

Services—Credit cards, calling cards, banking services, internet services, airline, hotels

Institutional/public service advertisements
Other

2. Roles of Women

1. Mother—woman shown with children visually
2. Wife/girlfriend—woman and man shown together (for "equality")
3. Friend—two or more women
4. Career—woman in business setting
5. Celebrity—movie star
6. Decorative—woman shown without a context merely to look pretty
7. Western model
8. Other

3. Presence of Male

1. Yes
2. No

4. Relationship with Male

1. Serving—woman shown serving tea, etc. to the male
2. Being served—woman being served by man
3. Equality—woman and man shown as partners/companions
4. Other

5. Dress Code

1. Dupatta/scarf present—traditional form of clothing—*shalwar kameez*—where it lies around the neck or over the shoulder.
2. Dupatta/scarf absent—modern form of clothing where the dupatta is not visible. The model is wearing Western clothes, for instance, sleeveless tops, jeans, etc.
3. Dupatta as prop—the dupatta is visible but only as a decorative accessory in the background or lap of the model, i.e., not on her figure per se.
4. Other—the presence of the dupatta is not discernable, etc.

APPENDIX B

Table 8.1
Demographic Profile of Women, Pakistan 2003

	WOMEN (%)	MEN (%)
Literacy rate	34.8	58.5
Primary Enrollment	35.2	58.2
Combined primary & secondary education	18	29
Urban literacy rate	56	69
Labor force	6.9	67
Top managerial posts	0.23	29.49

Source: Ministry of Women Development, Sindh

Table 8.2
Roles Played by Women in Advertisements in Urdu and English Magazines in Pakistan

ROLE	ENGLISH N	%	URDU N	%	TOTAL N	%
1 Decorative	209	49	106	53	315	50
2 Wife	62	15	28	14	90	14
3 Mother	47	11	42	21	89	14
4 Celebrity	37	9	16	8	53	8
5 Western	31	7	1	0.5	32	5
6 Friend	24	6	3	1	27	4
7 Other	11	3	4	2	15	2
8 Career	3	1	1	0.5	4	1
Total	424	100	201	100	625	100

Table 8.3
Products Advertised in Magazine Advertisements in Pakistan

PRODUCTS	N	%
1 Beauty and personal care	215	35
2 Food and food products	138	23
3 Pharmaceutical products	80	13
4 Women's clothing	50	8
5 Home furnishing, domestic appliances	45	7
6 Women's accessories	31	5
7 Services	24	4
8 Other	23	4
Total	606	100

Table 8.4
Male/Female Relationship in Magazine Advertisements in Pakistan

RELATIONSHIP	N	%
1 Beauty and personal care	215	35
1 Equality	87	85
2 Other	11	11
3 Serving	3	3
4 Being served	1	1
Total	102	100

Table 8.5
Dress Code of Women in Ads in English and Urdu Magazines in Pakistan

	ENGLISH		URDU		TOTAL	
DRESS CODE	N	%	N	%	N	%
1 Dupatta present	173	42	123	62	296	49
2 Dupatta absent	198	49	61	31	259	43
3 Other	20	5	14	7	34	6
4 Dupatta as prop	17	4	0	0	17	3
Total	408	100	198	100	606	100

Table 8.6
Roles of Women on TV in Pakistan

ROLES	PAKISTAN TELEVISION (State)		GEO TELEVISION (Private)	
	N	%	N	%
Wife/Girlfriend	49	47.1	50	49
Mother	39	37.5	13	12.7
Decorative	12	11.5	25	24.5
Friend	11	10.6	5	4.9
Career woman	7	6.7	3	2.9
Celebrity	6	5.8	11	10.8
Western Model			2	2
Others			1	1

Table 8.7
Products Advertised on TV in Pakistan

PRODUCTS	PAKISTAN TELEVISION (State)		GEO TELEVISION (Private)	
	N	%	N	%
Food and beverage	36	34.6	32	31.4
Beauty and personal care	27	26.0	5	4.9
Pharmaceutical	14	13.7	3	2.9
Institutional/Public service	12	11.8	2	2.0
Household cleaning	5	4.8	0	0
Domestic appliances/ Home furnishings	0	0	37	36.3
Automobiles	0	0	9	8.8
Services	5	4.8	10	9.8
Others	5	4.8	4	3.9
Total	104		102	

Table 8.8
Male/Female Relationship in Pakistan TV Ads

RELATIONSHIP	PAKISTAN TELEVISION (State)		GEO TELEVISION (Private)	
	N	%	N	%
Female serving	1	1.8	1	1.9
Female advising	8	14.6	0	0
Male/Female equal	44	80	46	86.8
Others	2	3.6	6	11.3
Total	55	100	53	100

REFERENCES

Ahmed, A. S. (1999). *Islam today: A short introduction to the Muslim world.* London. New York: I. B. Taurus.

Ansari, M. (2001). In Pakistan journalists maintain women's lesser status. *Nieman Reports.* Downloaded April 10, 2004, from http://www.nieman.harvard.edu/? reports/01-4NRwinter/92–93.pdf.

Asian Development Bank. (July 2000). *Women in Pakistan* [Country Briefing Paper]. Retrieved February 10, 2004, from http://www.adb.org/Documents/Books/? Country_Briefing_Papers/Women_in_Pakistan/prelims.pdf.

Barraclough, S. (2001). Pakistani television politics in the 1990s. *Gazette, 63*(2–3), 225–239.

Bose, S., & Jalal, A. (2004). *Modern South Asia: History, culture, political economy.* New Delhi: Oxford University Press.

Facts about GEO. (2005). Downloaded October 14, 2005, from http://www.geo.tv/.

Ilahi, H. (2001). Women should be portrayed in assertive roles on TV. Retrieved April 10, 2004, from http://www.dawn.com/2001/12/01/nat31.htm.

Mumtaz, K., & Shaheed, F. (1987). *Women of Pakistan: Two steps forward, one step back?* Lahore: Vanguard Books.

National policy for development and empowerment of women. Retrieved May, 12, 2004, from http://www.pakistan.gov.pk/women-development-division/ policies/nw-policy-03.html.

Orient Blue Book. (2002). Karachi: Orient McCann Erickson.

PEMRA Rules. (2002). Retrieved October 15, 2007, from http://www.pemra.gov.pk/ rules.html.

Siu, W., & Au, K. (1997). Women in advertising: A comparison of television advertisements in China and Singapore. *Marketing Intelligence and Planning, 15*(5), 235–243.

AUTHOR INDEX

SUBJECT INDEX

Printed in the United States
203985BV00001B/94-180/P